COOLING CUPS
&
DAINTY DRINKS

COOLING CUPS
&
DAINTY DRINKS

Classic Cocktail and Punch Recipes
for the Discerning Drinker

by

WILLIAM TERRINGTON

DUCKWORTH OVERLOOK

This edition published in 2017
by Duckworth Overlook

LONDON
30 Calvin Street, London E1 6NW
T: 020 7490 7300
E: info@duckworth-publishers.co.uk
www.ducknet.co.uk

For bulk and special sales please contact
sales@duckworth-publishers.co.uk

First published by George Routledge & Sons in 1869

Typeset in Caslon by M Rules

Printed and bound in Great Britain by
T J International Ltd, Padstow, Cornwall

9780715651315

1 3 5 7 9 10 8 6 4 2

FOREWORD

When I was asked to write the foreword for *Cooling Cups and Dainty Drinks* by William Terrington I was surprised. But, well, why not? I'd just had my own cocktail book, *Mixing in the Right Circles*, published in December 2016, taking a step which I felt was right for me after so many years of being behind the bar.

My style of bartending has been classically led, and the mixing of (mostly) spirits is second nature to me. As a rule, I'm not known for using juices and other mixers. My drinks are short and to the point. Straight up or on the rocks is me all over. I always admired the likes of William "Only William" Schmidt, and I could see Terrington being an influence on him and those that followed him.

Terrington was an interesting man who was less well known than the other "star bartenders" of his time, but he was no less important on the cocktail scene of the day.

The other thing about Terrington is that he might not have existed at all. It might have been a nom de plume for someone else. Perhaps a publisher, or a woman? So we've got a mystery here.

I spoke with my friends Anistasia Miller and Jared Brown, who are well-known cocktail historians and the authors of many cocktail and spirit-related books. Jared is also the master distiller for Sipsmith Gin.

He told me that Anistasia and he had spent "more time than you could imagine" searching through birth, death and voter records, as well as newspapers. "There doesn't seem to be a single person with his name or any logical variant of it in London the whole time he was supposed to be alive. It was not uncommon for publishers to use a nom de plume to give a bit more gravitas to a book."

According to Bernard Barbuck, cocktail historian, the section on wine is "riddled" with misinformation – already in the first paragraph, Terrington confuses a type of soil with a wine-growing area (Palus) and two regions (St Julien and St Estèphe) with châteaux – but his book "still has charm".

So there we have it: there is intrigue and controversy about Terrington, but also a lot of useful information in *Cooling Cups and Dainty Drinks*.

It was the first book published in Britain to contain recipes for both cocktails and cordials, and this made it ideal for the novice to try them out at home. His recipes for cordials are still relevant and most can be followed today without killing anybody. His mention of Oleo Saccharum, the process for drawing out the fat or oils from citrus, is just one example of a technique that is still used today.

His take on cocktails is high on whimsy and poetic at the same time.

He writes: "Cocktails are compounds very much used by 'early birds' to fortify the inner man, and by those who like their consolations hot and strong. 'Cocktail' is not so ancient an institution as Juleps, &c, but, with its next of kin, 'Crusta,' promises to maintain its ground."

I especially like his entry on Juleps. Of this class of drinks, he writes that the "nectarous compound 'Mint Julep' is the most popular in this country. It is an especial favourite with the Americans, especially down South. It was first brought into vogue here by Captain Marryat, who, in his work on America, says :—'I must descant a little upon the mint julep, as it is, with the thermometer a 100°, one of the most delightful and insinuating potations that ever was invented, and may be drunk with equal satisfaction when the thermometer is as low as 70°.'"

His recipe for a whisky julep is one I wish I'd written. "Put a few tops of mint into a tumbler; add 2 tablespoon-fuls of sugar and 3 of water; ¼ pint of whisky ; thin peel of a quarter of a lemon; in five minutes fill up with shaven ice; in drinking use straws, or a stick of maccaroni."

Refrigeration – something we take for granted nowa-days – is also touched on. Terrington writes: "An excellent mode of preserving ice for domestic use is by the refrigerator (or portable ice-chest); the possession of a good refrigera-tor, as regards the amount of comfort and luxury it brings, cannot be over-estimated; for icing wines and beverages it has special advantage, the temperature can be adjusted at pleasure, while the contents are not wasted or spoiled." He even recommends a brand he likes: "Those of the Wenham Lake Ice Company [of 140 The Strand, London] (who first introduced them into Britain in 1845) are both trustworthy and of excellent workmanship. This company has recently introduced an excellent vessel called 'The American Double Wall Ice-Water Pitcher' which is suitable for claret and all kinds of cups and cool beverages."

He has a technique for making Snow Ice: "Break some lake ice into small pieces, wrap them in a coarse strong cloth, and pound the mass into snow." He then goes on with more advice – how to make Ice Planes for juleps and cobblers, and how to freeze ice, which becomes quite scientific, so you had to know what you were doing.

When you really get into *Cooling Cups and Dainty Drinks* it's impressive to read how many subjects it covers. Today we are used to seeing boutique gins, beers, essences, oils and cordials of every flavour everywhere. Looks like the best things are still inspired by the past and made relevant again today.

Brian Silva
Manager of Covent Garden's Balthazar and author of *The Cocktail Book: Mixing in the Right Circles*

PREFACE

The original intention of the writer of this work was to produce a guide for the preparation of that now very prevalent kind of beverage called Cups, which should comprise a copious collection of recipes for that delicious class of drinks, to the study of which he has devoted no small portion of his time and attention.

In the course of his labours to this end, he found, however, that it was impracticable to restrict himself within the prescribed limits. The subject grew imperceptibly in his hands; and it became evident that if he adhered to his first plan, his book would be crowded with so many notes appertaining to Wines, Liqueurs, and other matters, as greatly to interfere with the simplicity of the design. He resolved, therefore, to extend the scope of the work, and to offer to the public a handbook treating of all the Beverages in modern use. He thinks it right to point out, however, that, as the principal object of the book is to furnish a collection of the most approved recipes for the making of Cups (treated of in detail in the Second Part of the work), the earlier portion, containing useful information on the subject of Wines, &c, should be regarded rather as introductory to a proper knowledge of the ingredients from which they are formed than as a special treatise on those Beverages.

Modern usage has considerably altered the social habits in vogue with our forefathers in both eating and drinking. All that was heavy, formal, and monotonous in their feasts has, owing to the more genial customs we have been led to adopt through our constant intercourse with France and other countries, given way to the display of a more refined taste; and this departure from old-fashioned ways in the selection of edibles has naturally led to a change no less beneficial in our bibulous doings. It is owing, however, to our extended acquaintance with the finer sorts of Wine, and a nicer discrimination in the choice and order of drinking them, but still more to the abandonment of the vicious old practice of sitting for hours after dinner to indulge in heavy libations, that we may attribute much of that change in our taste to which we have adverted. May we not ascribe to the same cause the relish for Claret Cup, and other beverages of a similar character, which has grown up amongst us? Some of these preparations are, indeed, of a flavour so exquisite, that the epicure may well be tempted to exclaim—

"One sip will bathe the drooping spirit in delight
beyond the bliss of dreams."

In a work purporting to touch upon every kind of Beverage, the reader will, of course, expect to find some account of the varied category of American drinks—of those Transatlantic "notions"—many of which, owing to their racy character, are properly styled "Sensations" by our Yankee cousins. We can promise that in this respect he will have no reason to be dissatisfied. A choice collection of these is given, the greater part of which well deserve the celebrity that attaches to them; and, as an occasional relish, all may claim to be regarded as both wholesome and exhilarating.

It is, perhaps, needless to add that *Ponche à la Romaine*, and the other varieties of the national beverage of Punch, as well as the important items of Ale, Beer, and Cider, are duly treated of in these pages.

The author has also given especial attention to the subject of Refrigeration—almost a new art among us—as well as to that of aërated waters, and other draughts so much sought after in the summer season. Useful information is also afforded on the subject of Tea, Coffee, Cocoa, and other *cups* of the temperate order, as well as on certain liqueurs made with their aid.

In conclusion, he trusts that his manual of *Cooling Cups and Dainty Drinks* may be found to convey much sound information on beverages of all kinds, and that it may be deemed a not unworthy companion of the better class of works devoted to the pleasant topic of Good Cheer.

CONTENTS

PART I:
GENERAL BEVERAGES

WINES

ALCOHOL

LIQUEURS AND SYRUPS

BITTER DRINKS

ALE AND BEER

REFRIGERATION

TEMPERATE BEVERAGES

ESSENCES AND SPICES USED IN MAKING CUPS

PART II:
CUPS, AND SOCIAL DRINKS

WINE CUPS

---

* The letter A attached to this and several of the succeeding articles denotes that they are American drinks; and when the letter E is appended, that they are English.

PUNCH

PART I

General Beverages

WINES

Wine, that glorious juice of the grape, elegantly designated by an ancient poet as a recompense given for the miseries incurred by mankind through the Deluge, has puzzled poets and historians in all ages to account satisfactorily for its discovery. It has been ascribed to Noah, and many other ancient celebrities, but its origin has been accounted for in so misty and vague a manner, and accompanied by circumstances so fabulous, that we forbear all attempts at unravelling the web of its ancient history, and propose to come at once to a description of its best-known varieties, and of the chief characteristics of those kinds with which we are now most familiar.

The Vine, which is a native of the middle regions of the temperate zone, has been an object of culture from the earliest ages, and its history is inseparably connected with those countries where it flourishes. It is capable of producing many varieties of wines, possessing different qualities, the result of peculiarities of soil and climate, as well as of the aspect it presents to the sun, and other causes, many of which are not yet well ascertained. Thus it happens that one vineyard, perhaps separated from the next by merely a few stakes, and without particular difference of soil, culture, or aspect, may produce a far superior wine to its neighbour. Sir Emerson Tennant tells us, that,—"The finest known wines are the produce of soils the combination and proportions of whose ingredients are extremely rare and exceptional; and cooperating with these, they require the agency of peculiar degrees of light, moisture, and heat. The richest wine of France, Italy, Hungary, Madeira, and Teneriffe are grown on the sites of extinct volcanoes." If proof be required of the value of the adage, "not to trust to appearances," we would recommend a visit to some of the celebrated vine-lands of Europe; for example, those of Médoc, near Bordeaux, where the traveller's classical associations connected with the vine would be much disturbed on viewing the cropped and stunted expanse of bushes attached to low espaliers rising about two feet from the ground, and producing grapes which look like over-ripe black currants. Yet these unpromising grapes are those which produce the renowned wines of Lafite and Château Margaux, worth, at least, ten shillings a bottle. It seems an established fact that the fruit of vines highly grown are not so productive as the fruit of low-trained plants; and in observing the usages of the ancients, it is surprising how small is the change that the lapse of time has brought into the culture of" the vine in Italy. It appears the plant is still grafted and managed there as it was in the days of Varro, author of *De Re Rustica*, who died 28 B.C. In other countries where the culture of the grape has been more scientifically treated, the varieties have been astonishingly multiplied; but in Italy the vines are allowed to follow their natural mode of growth, and are simply trained picturesquely amongst trees and on trellis-work.

Let us now direct our attention to the glorious vintage-season, the annual festival of Médoc,—October, "the wine month," as it is called,—when the ruby tears of the grape are made into the most delicious beverage—a wine destined to find a welcome at the halls and palaces of wealthy epicures in various countries. For weeks previously, the weather is anxiously watched from day to day; for upon a continuance of weeks of fine weather the savour and *bouquet* of the wine essentially depend. Warmed by the glare of an unclouded sun, tempered by mild westerly winds, and moistened by dews, the grapes ripen and attain their exquisite flavour. When all is ready for the gathering, everyone is astir. The contents of the vehicles which come loaded from the vineyard are no sooner deposited in the *cuvier*, or wine-press, than the treaders jump in and proceed to stamp out the purple juice, standing in it almost up to their knees. The wine-press consists of shallow tubs of different sizes, with holes in the side level with the bottom, from which the juice runs out, and passing through a sieve is strained from the husks into vessels below, ready to receive it. The treaders continue thus employed till all the juice has passed through into the vessels below. It takes nearly an hour to tread out all the juice from a good-sized *cuvier*; the juice is then emptied from the receiving vessels into large vats, and the residue remaining in the *cuvier* is added to the juice in the vats. When these are sufficiently full, the fermentation proceeds; and so powerful is the emanation of carbonic acid gas, that no one can enter farther than the doorway. There the listener may hear strange bubblings solemnly echoing in the cool and dark hall, and which proclaim that a great change is taking place,—that these vats of mawkish, sweet, juice are being converted into noble and generous wine. There is something wonderful in this mysterious change. Nature will have no intrusion during her mystic operations. The atmosphere around and near the vats would be death to any who should venture near, fenced in, as the vats are, during the grand transmutation by a halo of stifling carbonic gas.

The French are generally considered the best vine-cultivators in the world. The process of wine-treading is pursued very generally in France, being considered superior, in many vine districts, to the employment of mechanical squeezing. But this last process is used for expressing the juice of the grape for the sparkling wines of Champagne, and it is also the case in Germany.

The wines known in France as *Vins de Bordeaux*, are with us classed under the general name of *Claret*, a name signifying that it is a mixed wine of a clear red colour,—

> "Claret, sweet as the lips we press,
> In sparkling fancy, as we drain the bowl."

The district in which these wines are produced was the ancient province of Gascony (now the department of the

Gironde), and is estimated to possess above 37,000 acres of vineyard, thickly planted, and constituting one of the most valuable wine districts in France. The popularity of Claret has fluctuated very much in this country, but it now promises to become as common in England as it was nearly two hundred years ago, when our hostility to Louis XIV and his policy resulted in breaking off, as far as possible, all commercial relations with our neighbours, and led to the introduction of the red wines of Portugal, for the avowed purpose of superseding the use of Claret and Burgundy. Claret was much esteemed in England during the noontide of chivalry, when the Black Prince kept court at Bordeaux. Froissart says that, on one occasion, a fleet of 200 merchant-men came from England to Bordeaux for wine. In process of time, however, the Bordeaux wines were superseded in England by the sack produced in Spain and the Canaries, which, with the wines of the Rhine, held sway till the Stuarts again brought Claret in, and, long after the differential duty imposed on it by the Union, it was the favourite potable of the Scotch.

Claret is divided into several classes, rated according to their excellence. The chief vine tracts are those of Médoc, Graves, Palus, and Blanche, each particular vineyard producing a peculiar sort of vine; that of Médoc yielding the glorious vintage of Château Margaux, Lafite, Latour, and others, such as Léoville, Larose, St. Julien, St. Estèphe, Branne Mouton, and other celebrated red wines. The famous *Haut Brion* is produced from the vine tract of Le Graves, which also produces the white wine known as *Vin-de-Grave*, The wines of the flat and fertile Palus are

deep-coloured, full-bodied, rough and hard, when new,
but they improve much by keeping. Being well adapted for
long voyages, they are known as cargo wines. The Blanches,
or dry white wine district, gives us the wines known as
Sauterne, Barsac, &c. Among the choice white wines produced in this district the most famous is *Château d'Yquem*.
This celebrated wine is now getting into great favour in this
country, and commands high prices. The generality of the
wines of Bordeaux, through containing little alcohol, will
stand and keep well. They are greatly improved by a sea
voyage; indeed it often happens that wines of a lower growth
will become so much improved as to almost equal the finer
growths. The characteristics of the best red growths are a
bright deep ruby or violet colour, exquisite bouquet, of the
flavour of the raspberry and violet, a soft silky taste to the
palate, and possessing the quality of endurance. Ordinary
claret is one of the most refreshing and invigorating of beverages. It is easy of digestion, and well suited for general
use, especially in warm climates, being a mildly stimulating
drink. The district has been estimated to produce upwards
of 85,000,000 gallons of wine.

Champagne.—Let us now turn to Champagne—"the
spring dew of the spirit—the heart's rain;" this is the produce of vineyards in the ancient province, so called, which
now comprehends the departments of Aube, Ardennes,
Marne, and Haut Marne: the surface of the country presents extensive plains with ranges of hills. The wines are
distinguished, according to the site of the vineyards, into
river or mountain growths, the former being for the most
part white, the latter red. The vineyards in the department

of Marne produce the most esteemed wines, those of the neighbourhood of Epernay and Rheims being the most famous among them, Epernay, which is situated between hills in the midst of the vine-lands, may be designated the head-quarters of Champagne; for here, and in its immediate vicinity, is the best vine-land, the most extensive cellarage, and the finest palatial residences of the more eminent manufacturers. The cellarage of one firm alone, that of "Möet and Chandon," is said to be five miles in extent, all cut out of the calcareous rock, and containing on an average 5,000,000 bottles of wine. There are other cellars equalling the above-named for vastness and capacity, and in them is stowed the wine of manufacturers whose names and brands are known to the whole civilized world. Champagne, being better known by the name of the makers than by the designation of the vineyards that produce it, with the exception of a few choice growths among the white, is the produce of the old vineyard "Sillery," anciently known as *Vin de la Maréchale*. This wine is of an amber hue, exquisite bouquet, with a clear pleasant dry taste; and the wines of Ay are sparkling, bright, and possess a peculiarly pine-apple aroma. Those of Mareuil, Hautvilliers, Pierry, Epernay, and some others, are, with the choice red growths of Verzy, Verzenay, Bouzy, &c, much sought after by connoisseurs; but the Red (or Mountain Champagne) wines, though of good colour and body, are, on the whole, less esteemed than the white. The Pink ("*Champagne rose*") differs only in the manufacture from those which are colourless. Sparkling Champagne (*grand mousseux*) is the result of incomplete fermentation, and, being the most sparkling, and invariably the brightest, is very captivating; but it is not the choicest, the confined carbonic acid holding the wine in the volatile state so much desired. It has not the peculiar bouquet in so marked a degree as the creaming or slightly sparkling wine (*crémens*, or *demi-mousseux*). The wine most esteemed by connoisseurs is the "still," so called by reason of its being bottled after the fermentation has ceased, thereby constituting it a more natural, and, therefore, more wholesome wine.

Champagne wine has been recommended by the faculty as a valuable medicine for keeping up the system during exhaustion. It contains more or less carbonic acid, the result of which is to carry off the effect of the spirit, and to stimulate the system, without subsequent depression. It contains little mucilaginous matter, and, being a thin wine, is easily digested. As a stimulus, it is the least injurious; while, as a tonic, it ranks much lower than most other wines. Bad or fictitious Champagne is highly injurious to health; hence the importance of judgment in the selection and purchase of this wine, all not being Champagne that is represented as such. The brands and names of the best manufacturers being closely imitated, a good test of genuine Champagne is the rapidity with which it throws down its head; hence the desirability of using a tall glass, in preference to the flat broad glasses now so much in vogue. Good Champagne does not require much iceing. Mr. Brande tells us: "The prevalent notion, that a glass of Champagne cannot be too quickly swallowed is erroneous; and it is no bad test of the quality of Champagne to have it exposed for some time in a wine-glass, when, if originally of the highest order, it will be found to have lost its carbonic acid gas, but to have retained its body and flavour, which had before been concealed by its effervescence. Champagne, therefore, should not be drunk till this active effervescence is over, by those who would relish the above characteristic quality."

The Champagne district is estimated to produce annually on an average 52,000,000 gallons of wine. The manufacturers sustain much loss from the bursting of bottles. That, and the care demanded in the manufacture, and expense entailed before a bottle is ready to be sent to market, renders genuine Champagne an expensive wine. Champagne intended for the English market is much drier than that intended for the American and Russian. The French take wine excessively iced, and drink Champagne towards the close of dinner. This wine first attained the great celebrity it still enjoys in the seventeenth century, but it was noted as a first-class wine in the thirteenth century (see *Bataille des Vins*). Adjoining the district of Champagne, in the South (and indeed a continuation of the same wine tract), is the ancient province of the Dukes of Burgundy—*les princes des bons vins*. Its vineyards produce the glorious wine known as *Burgundy*—"with all its sunlight glow."

This wine during the last century provoked a redoubtable controversy between the professors of physic and men of science of the time. The dispute, which related to the comparative merits of Burgundy and Champagne, lasted for nearly a century, when a solemn decree was pronounced by the Faculty of Medicine in favour of Champagne ; a verdict which certainly was not agreed to by the great Napoleon, whose favourite drink was Chambertin, a celebrated kind of Burgundy. Some of the vines in the celebrated vineyard of Clos-de-Vougeôt are said to be 300 years old. This wine, with Romanée Conti, Richebourg, La Tache, Corton, Beaune, Volnay, Pommard, and some others, all rank as delicious, delicate wines. The best Burgundy for travelling is Corton, which is a sound, enduring wine. Macon and Beaujolais are also good wines. Of the white Burgundies, the best known are Montrachet (so celebrated for its high perfume), Meursalt, the beautiful amber colour of the Goutte d'Or, and Chablis, which is a white, dry, flinty-tasting wine. Burgundy wines are in much request in France. The district is estimated to produce annually 75,000,000 gallons. The produce is classified into growths, as those of Haute Bourgogne, Basse Bourgogne, and Côte d'Or; this last producing the choicest growths. Burgundy is stronger than Claret, and possesses an exquisite aroma, which, with its delicious flavour, crown it in the estimation of epicures as the very King of Wines.

Descending the Rhône, passing the St. Péray district, which yields wine of no mean order, we come to the vicinity of the town of Tain, where is grown one of the finest wines France produces, the celebrated and scarce White and Red *Hermitage*. These wines derive that name from the ruins of an old hermitage that still exists on the summit of the hill on whose slopes are planted the vines which yield the choicest quality. Red Hermitage is highly regarded for its full body, dark purple colour, exquisite perfume and flavour; but its brilliant colour sensibly fades after it has been kept twenty years. There are five classes of Hermitage wine (as the production of all the immediate district is named); the best, or *Ermitage paille*, is very choice and expensive.

Côte Rôti is a generous red clear wine, with a slight bitter taste, and violet bouquet.

Gauphine is sound, useful wine, grown in the Hérault. Roussillon, on the borders of the Mediterranean, produces some of the deepest-coloured and fullest-bodied of French wines. One of them, *Masdeu* (which is the name for God's field or vineyard), is a full-bodied, bright, red wine, with a bouquet not unlike Claret, yet partaking of a Port character; in fact, so much like Port, that a good deal of it is sold and used in England as Port. It was the red wines of Roussillon which formed the basis of the famous Bristol Ports, so well-known in the last century.

In proximity to Masdeu, come the rich, luscious wines Frontignac, Rivesaltes, Lunel, and many others, but little known in this country. On the seaboard of this district, 15 miles S.W. of Montpellier is the port and town of Cette, famous as the great manufacturing depôt of fictitious wines and liqueurs.

We will now visit another land,—

"Where the Rhine his course does bend,
Rich vine-covered hills among."

The Rhine and the Vine have for centuries been associated together, and the Germans are as fond of their wines as they are of their river, which they fondly call the Father of Wine. That glorious river, with its majestic beauty and vine-clad banks, offers to the admiration of the traveller a lovelier scene than any other river can present; more especially along its course between Mentz and Coblentz. The choicest vintages are confined to a small district called the Rheingau, which extends from Rüdesheim to Mentz. The vine-tract of Hochheim, a village situated on the river Main, producing wines of like nature and excellence, which are classed with the Rhine growths. These wines are extensively imported into this country, and it would seem that this last-mentioned kind especially, has, by our abbreviation of its name to "Hock," served as a familiar designation with us of all Rhenish wines. Of the growths of the district of the Rheingau, which is 10 miles long by about 14 broad, the choicest is Schloss (or castle of) Johannisberg. This is a rare "cabinet wine," and has been famous for centuries; it is produced close under the walls of the old abbey of Johannisberg. The old monks had an especial regard for their vineyard, and were very chary of its produce. For several years past the estate has belonged to Prince Metternich, who showed that he appreciated his much-envied 62 acres of vineyard, by the care he caused to be exercised on its yield. Curiously, the vines which produce the *crème de la crème* of Johannisberg grow over and near the cellars. A worthy rival of this precious wine is Steinberg, also a "cabinet wine," the production of 108 acres of vine-land which belongs to the Duke of Nassau. This wine is the strongest of all Rhine wines. Both these wines are very choice and costly. Rüdesheim is also a choice wine, and the vineyard producing it is said to have been planted by Charlemagne; Geisenheim, Markobrunn, Rothenberg, and a few others, which are all well known and distinguished for their choice growths. These wines, which are all white, are soft and delicate in flavour. The best red Rhine wine is grown at Asmannshausen, a village about two miles N.W. of Rüdesheim, but the quantity produced is small. This wine was famed as far back as 1108. The durability of the wines of the Rhine is remarkable. It is this excellent quality most probably that originated the singular custom of storing the Rhine wines in vessels of enormous magnitude, such as the great tun of Heidelberg (built in 1751), which was 30 feet in length and 20 in depth; and that of the Gruningen tun, 30 feet long by 18 in diameter; also the tun of Tübingen, 24 feet long by 16 in diameter, and many others of sizes closely approaching those named, it being a great point of rivalry amongst the wine proprietors to produce these huge vessels, which were always kept full, either by replacing each quantity drawn with the like quantity of wine of a similar strength, or by adding washed pebbles to fill up the void. The peculiar qualities of these wines appear to form an exception to the prevalent chemical theories; their sharpness of flavour occasions a suspicion of acidity, yet they are highly agreeable, abounding in delicate aroma, and are also dry and sound, while they contain very little alcohol. "In a word," as Dr. Henderson remarks, "the wines of the Rhine may be regarded as constituting a distinct order by themselves. Some of the higher sorts, indeed, resemble very much the Vins de Grave, but in general they are drier than the French white wines, and are characterized by a delicate flavour and aroma, called in the country *gare*, which is quite peculiar to them, and of which it would be in vain to attempt the description. A notion prevails that they are naturally acid; and the inferior kinds are no doubt so; but this is not the constant character of the Rhine wines, which in good years have not any perceptible acidity to the taste—at least, not more than is common to them, with the growth of warmer regions. But their chief distinction is their extreme durability, in which they are not surpassed by any other species of wine." Of this durability an interesting anecdote is told. In the autumn of 1800, Lord Nelson left the Mediterranean, and, on his way to England, stopped at Hamburg. A wine-merchant, seventy years of age, who had some highly prized Rhine wine of the vintage of 1625, which had been in his keeping fifty years, felt desirous to bestow some on an extraordinary occasion, and present it to some celebrated and worthy personage. Accordingly, he asked Lord Nelson to accept six dozen of this matchless wine, hoping that part of it would have the honour to mix with the heart's blood of the hero. Nelson took the old gentleman kindly by the hand, but would only accept six bottles; twelve were sent, and the hero remarked he hoped to have so many victories, so as to drink his Hamburg friend's health with a bottle after each. An effervescing wine is made from the lower Rhine growths, but it has not any recommendable merit except cheapness, not having the quality of good Rhenish, or the rich fine flavour of Champagne, which it endeavours to imitate. Whoever desires a sound, honest wine, which will impart cheerfulness instead of pressing on the brain, yet a wine of delicate aroma containing very little alcohol, let him drink Rhenish wine.

The wine designated "Liebfraumilch," made in the vicinity of Worms, is an excellent wine. Many other valuable wines are produced on the banks of the Necker and other rivers which flow into the Rhine, and are known by the name of the locality where they are grown.

Stein-wein (stone wine) is grown near Wurzburg-on-the-Main, in Franconia; also Leisten wein, which is esteemed one of the finest wines of the south of Germany, and being invariably reserved for the Royal Bavarian cellar, it can rarely be purchased.

The wines of the Rhine and Moselle share some general resemblance of flavour, but the latter will not keep so long as Rhenish wine, although a great deal of the produce from the "banks of the blue Moselle" is sold in this country as Hock. The most esteemed wines are Grünhäuser, "the nectar of the Moselle," Scharzberg, and Brauneberg. Scharzhofberg, made from selected grapes, is the finest produce of the Moselle vine-land. Sparkling Moselle, of which great quantities come to the English market, is made principally from under-ripe grapes. The great peculiarity of the Moselle wines is their musk-like or elder-flower-like bouquet; this is imparted artificially to the inferior growths, in order to imitate the flavour and aroma of the Muscat grape.

At Ehrenbreitstein, or "broad stone of honour," the famous fortress opposite the mouth of the Moselle, are stored in the cellars under the grammar school, 300 vats, which are estimated to contain 400,000 bottles of Moselle and Rhenish wines.

Port.—This wine, which is so identified with the social habits of this country, where it has formed the staple wine of our dinner-tables and desserts for the last 160 years, is produced from a district in Portugal called the Cima de Douro, or Alto Douro. The choicest vineyards are situated on a succession of hills on each side of the river Douro, distant about 50 miles from Oporto, from which place the wine

derives its name, *i.e.*, Porto, or Oporto wine. The vintage
season, which begins in September and ends in October,
is capable of producing, in favourable years, 70,000 pipes of
wine, each pipe averaging about 115 gallons. The vintages
are divided into separate classes, the principal being those
which are termed Factory wines (*vintros de Feitoria*), or
assorted wines for exportation to England, and "*vintros sep-
arados*," or assorted wines for home and other consumption.
Mr. Oswald Crawford, in his Consular Commercial Report,
gives the following account of Port wine-making:—"The
wine-making, though at first primitive, is in all essential
particulars very cautiously and skilfully performed. The
over-ripe or inferior grapes being picked out, the best are
thrown into a large stone-built vat (*lagar*). Into this as many
men as can easily find room enter and tread out the juice; the
must is then allowed to stand till a thorough fermentation
has taken place. It is now that a small portion of brandy is
added, as is also done with Sherry and Madeira, to prevent
the wine, containing, as it does, so many rich ingredients,
from running into an excessive fermentation, and so losing
much of its saccharine matter." From the rich nature of the
Douro grape, which, when hung up in the sun to dry, are
like masses of sugar, the fermentation, once begun, would
not stop of its own accord (even when the wine is drawn
away) till it becomes unpleasantly bitter; hence, to retain the
delicious qualities of the grape, it is necessary to add brandy
at the critical moment, ere the bitterness commences. The
colour of Port wine varies from a dark red to a deep tawny
brown when old. When it has become tawny, it loses much
of its astringency. It derives its colour from the skin of

the grape, without the aid of geropiga or any other foreign
ingredient:

> "How great the crime, how flagrant the abuse,
> T' adulterate generous wine with noxious juice."

Of the excellence of genuine Port wine many a travelling connoisseur can testify who has drunk it on the spot
and enjoyed the full mellow body, exquisite flavour, and
seducing mildness of the pure unmixed juice of the grape;
but after the " blending" and adulterations to which the
choice wines of the Alto Douro are subjected in order to
reduce them to the orthodox Port standard, it would be just
as reasonable to expect the product to be good as to hope to
increase the quantity of true Burgundy, of Clos Vougeôt or
Romanée Conti, by turning the inferior Vins du Pays into a
vat containing the precious wine of the province.

In the year 1703, a time when an angry feeling of hostility existed towards France, a commercial treaty was made
between England and Portugal, which became known
by the name of the ambassador who negotiated it as the
Methuen treaty. This compact gave the wines of Portugal
a decided advantage in the English markets, much to the
dislike of good judges of the period, whose favourite drink
was choice Claret, with sometimes a dash of Port in it. From
that date till the present time the use of Port wine has been
adopted almost as our national beverage, so that English
dinners were for a century and a half considered incomplete
without that orthodox wine.

The wines of Oporto, abounding as they do in an

astringent principle, are very often used medicinally. Professor Brande says, that "good Port wine duly kept is, when taken in moderation, one of the most wholesome of vinous liquors: it strengthens the muscular system, assists the digestive powers, accelerates the circulation, exhilarates the spirits, and sharpens the mental energies; but, when taken in excess, it is perhaps the most mischievous of wines, and most likely to produce those permanent derangements of the digestive organs which follow the habitual use of distilled spirits." The sediment usually seen in an old bottle of Port is formed by the bitartrate of potash (cream of tartar), which, being slightly soluble in wine, gradually settles, and forms what is known as "the crust." It is a good criterion of sound Port if on drawing the cork its under surface when dry presents small crystals of tartar. A dry wine is full in flavour, but not abounding in sweetness; while a full-bodied wine is generally newly made. Port wine is "blended" by the wine-merchants similar to the process observed with Sherry. There are, however, some choice vintages, well known to connoisseurs, that escape this doctoring, some of them having fetched enormous prices, as much as £35 per dozen having been given for Port wine of the year 1820. Mr. Beckwith says, with regard to the characteristics of Port, "it may be stated that a modified 'fruitiness' in it is an essential, but that it should never be *sweet*." Rich colour, firmness, homogeneousness, and a tendency to dryness, with some astringency, will not fail to be among the qualities of good Port wine. When, in addition to these, it has obtained a ripe age in bottle, and has acquired some bouquet, it is undeniably—whatever may be urged to the contrary—a noble and generous beverage, and among Englishmen will never fail to find admirers." The other best known of the Portuguese wines are Calcavella, a white, sweet, muscatel wine; Bucellas, also a white wine, made from vines transplanted from the Rhenish districts; and Lisbon wine : these two latter, which are rich and dry, are grown in and near Lisbon.

Sherry.—We now come to the well-known white wines of Spain, familiar to us under the designation of Sherry. They derive this name (an anglicized mode of pronouncing Xeres) from Xeres de la Frontera, a town in Andalusia, the frontier town of the Christians during the occupation of Cadiz by the Moors, from which port it is distant about 16 miles. Sherry, properly so called, is the produce of the vineyards of the triangular district formed by Xeres de la Frontera, Santa Maria, and San Lucar de Barrameda; the vine district is about 12 miles square, and watered by the rivers Guadalquivir and Guadalete. The fine dry wines of the Xeres district were well known in this country during the sixteenth and seventeenth centuries. The poets and writers of that period make frequent mention of this generous wine. Shakespeare, who no doubt had partaken of some, which Lord Essex brought home from the sacking of Cadiz in 1596, says: "Your Sherries warms the blood, which was before cold and settled, and left the liver white, which is the badge of pusillanimity, but the Sherries makes its course from the inwards to the parts extreme." The controversy amongst antiquarians and Shakespearian annotators concerning this wine is thus disposed of by Mr. Ford, who, in speaking of Sherris Sack, says, "The term used by Falstaff, no mean authority on this matter, is the precise 'Seco de Xeres,' the term by which the wine is known to this day in its own country. The epithet *seco* or dry, the sack of old English authors, and the *sec* of French ones, being used in contradistinction to the sweet malmseys and muscadels, which are also made of the same grape." The finest and driest sort of Xeres wine is Amontillado; and the peculiarity of its flavour is a mystery of nature that has not been correctly solved. When the farmer intends making this wine, the grapes are plucked about a fortnight before the general vintage, and the produce kept apart; out of 20 butts, however, it generally happens not above two will have the quality so much desired. Sometimes, as if by caprice, a butt of wine from the general vintage will assume the Amontillado flavour. Brandy added to Amontillado would ruin it, hence, coupled with Montilla, a fine wine grown near Cordova and Manzanilla, so called from the Spanish word for camomile, the flavour of which it yet partakes of. This trio is unapproachable as presenting fine, dry, pure, and healthy wines. All Xeres wines are, when unmingled with *arrope* (the Arabic word for boiled must), of a pale colour. The difference in the colour of Sherries is principally owing to the peculiar choice of the different palates to please which they are prepared. They are in general coloured with *arrope*, which is thus made: a butt of ordinary Sherry is boiled down to about one-fifth of its bulk, acquiring a deep brown colour, and according to the various tints or flavour desired; *arrope* is next added, with Brandy and Sweet Wine also, if required. Sherries should be judged by their taste, not by their colour; a pure wine will soon proclaim itself. Sherry, when pure, contains less free acid, it is not so stimulating as most wines, and agrees well with most constitutions. Dietetically speaking, it is becoming the wine in most general use in England. It is also much used as a pharmaceutical agent, for the extraction of the medicinal properties from some drugs which require spirit for their solution. Some idea may be conceived of the vast amount of wine stored in Xeres, when in the warehouse or bodegas of M. Domecq alone is on an average stored 15,000 butts of wine, each butt averaging 108 gallons, bottling from 50 to 52 dozen to the butt. These bodegas are large warehouses, very lofty and well ventilated, and are filled with tiers of 4 butts of wine (*soleras*). A visit to a bodega, especially if accompanied by the capitaz (or head man), will be found worthy of remembrance as one of an agreeable nature, especially so if his explanations are rendered more intelligible by a bumper drawn from the most ancient "Madre" butt, which invariably contains wine that is the accumulated produce of some 50 vintages. The wine-merchants of Xeres never export their stock of the oldest and finest wines, and in accordance with the price at which they are valued so the wines are compounded. Thus a butt of wine said to be 30 or 40 years old will contain a portion of the vintage of several seasons; for, as the wine is drawn from the butt, it is replenished by a contribution from the next in point of age and fineness, and so on through the bodegas. The workmen, inclusive of the capitaz employed, are chiefly from the mountains of the Asturias, and, as soon as they have acquired sufficient to retire upon, go back to their mountain homes. The Xeres grape has been planted in many places, but nowhere does it produce such fine wine as it does in its own native soil.

The principal sweet and coloured Andalusian wines are known by the name of Paxarette and Rota Tente; this last is used as a sacramental wine. There are, besides, many excellent white and red Spanish wines, among the latter of which we should mention *Val de Peñas*, resembling Burgundy; it is made near Manzanares. Sherry wines are known in England by the names of the shippers: the brands of Domecq, Gonzales, Dubosc & Co., Cozens, and others, are towers of strength. Sherry is less adulterated than most wines. It is estimated that the annual wine produce of Spain averages upwards of 136,000,000 of gallons.

Sherry is improved by being decanted not less than two hours before it is required for use.

Madeira, the produce of the island so called, is a first-class wine, darker than Sherry; it was not much known till the latter end of the seventeenth century; since its introduction it has been extensively sought after and much esteemed of late years. The supply of this wine has fallen off; in 1856 there was none made, owing to the prevalence of the *oïdium*, or vine-scourge, which first made its appearance in this island, eventually destroying all the vines. It is supposed that it will take several years for the perfect restoration of the vineyards. The meaning of the terms "East and West India Madeira" signifies that the wine has made a voyage from the island to one or the other of these parts, by which process the effect of decomposing the saccharine principle is accelerated, and the wine moreover becomes ripened, by passing through a warmer climate. The wine selected for this purpose, usually the sort called "London Particular," is shipped in butts, and remains either on board or is landed at one of the Indian ports for a time, and is then reshipped for the London market or whatever country it is destined for. That which has been to the East Indies is considered, by virtue of the greater heat of the climate, and the length of the voyage, to have a softer flavour than the West India Madeira.

Malmsey Madeira is a very choice rich wine, and capable of being kept many years. It is produced from a grape which will only flourish on a small spot in Madeira—the valley of the Câmara de Lobos, on the south of the island. Old Sherry and old Madeira rank very high as perfect wines. They ought to be destitute of acidity and astringency, but stimulating and nourishing, these qualities being so nicely proportioned that the spirit they contain assists their digestion. It is principally on these grounds that they constitute an excellent beverage for the dyspeptic, the sedentary, and the invalid generally. It is of this class of wines, especially of Canary, that Howell spoke more than two and a half centuries ago: "If of any others may be verified the merry induction that good wine maketh good blood, good blood causeth good humours, good humours cause good thoughts, good thoughts bring forth good works, good works carry a man to heaven: *ergo*, good wine carries a man to heaven. If this be true, more English go to heaven than any other, for I think there is more Canary brought to England than the world besides."

Marsala resembles Madeira in colour, and somewhat in flavour. It is a sound, useful, and reasonable wine, made in the Island of Sicily. It was originally produced at Bronté, on an estate which belonged to Lord Nelson. When well aged, it is a really good wholesome wine, and deserves to be better known, being far superior to much that passes under the name of Sherry.

Malaga is chiefly a dry wine, similar to Sherry, but much inferior to it in flavour, being sweet-tasted. Many of the wines of Malaga are brought to Santa Maria, Cadiz, and shipped from thence, under the name of Sherry. Most of the common Sherries are of this class, or San Lucar growth. There are three vintages in Malaga; the first in June, producing a rich sweet wine; the next in October, producing a species of Sherry; while the November gatherings are termed mountain wines, being sweet, luscious, and dry. They are both red and white.

Benicarlos is a red wine, produced from the vine-land surrounding Benicarlo, in Valencia. It is much used for "blending" with other red wines, especially Bordeaux. A great deal of the cheap sorts of Port is manufactured from this wine. About 220,000 casks are annually exported for this purpose; a great deal of it goes to Cette.

Alicante, of which the best wines are the Alogne and Tent, both much liked in Spain, produces a considerable quantity of wine, much used for blending with the produce of France and other parts. Of the vines of Catalonia, some, such as Tarragona, when of good age, are excellent, red, good-bodied wines. The produce of this district is much used for "blending" with the wines of Oporto.

The wines of Italy are very numerous, and are made principally for home consumption. The sparkling wines differ from those of other countries, being less effervescing. Of this class, Asti (red and white), Nebiola, Passeretta, rank first. The wines of Bologna are in general sparkling wines, known as Vino Crudoe. There are also some boiled wines, but they are not much known. The best red wines are Lambrusco, Barbera, Aleatico; and of the white, Malvasia (vinto Santo), and the delicious Lachrymae Christi, which is grown at Mont Somma, near Vesuvius. This wine is both rare and choice. It is of a muscatel character, having an agreeable bouquet, and a sweet piquant taste. Tuscany is deemed better as a wine district than any other part of Italy. The mode of bottling in Florence has given rise to the term "flask of wine;" these wine flasks being almost identical with those in which oil is imported, but they are made generally of larger size. Vermuth is a white wine, made aromatic with wormwood. This wine is much used as a stomachic. The best, which comes from Turin, is expensive.

Monte Fiascone is an aromatic intoxicating wine, made in the Roman States, while that named Vino Greco is a rich kind made in Naples, from the grape so called.

Although the wines of Italy are not much known in this country, it must not be supposed that the Italians cannot produce good wine, although they export very little.

The wines of Greece are good, sound, unbrandied, yet firm-bodied wines, and bid fair, through the steady advocacy of Mr. Denman, well known as the author of "The Vine and its Fruit," to become as generally appreciated in this country as they were during the medieval age, when these wines furnished an important beverage at the social gatherings of the time, under the name of Cyprus, Malmsey, or Malmesyne, so named from Malvagnia in the Morea, from whence the Malmsey grape originally came. Dr. Henderson tells us that "throughout nearly the whole of Greece the soil is highly favourable to the vine. On the Continent, the extensive range of mountains which intersect the country are chiefly calcareous. In those islands which have been celebrated for their general fertility and the superiority of their vines, Scio, Tenedos, Candia, Zante, &c, similar strata occur. In others, where the growths are of equal repute as Lesbos, Naxos, and Santorin—the Thera of the ancients—the rocks are of volcanic origin. The variety of climate, and choice exposures which the elevated ground presents, serve to diversify, to an infinite degree, the quality of the wines obtained." The wines of Santorin are excellent for keeping, and improve with age; those of Visanto, Lachrymae Christi, are sweet and luscious. St. Elie is a dry pale wine; while Thera, red and white Mont Hymet, and others, are worthy of attention as good honest wines.

Of the wines of Austria, the best generally known are those of Steinberg and Vöslauer, near Vienna. The excellent character of this wine is shown by the fact that large quantities were shipped on board the frigate "Novara," in her cruise round the world, which occupied two and a half years, and on her return, the remainder (300 bottles) was found to have much improved, in spite of the many changes of climate it had undergone. There are three varieties of this wine—red, white, sparkling. Dr. Druitt says: "The red Vöslauer is a good full-bodied, serviceable, and economical wine. Its stoutness renders it more satisfying than Bordeaux, at equal price. There is no complaint of thinness, coldness, or poverty. It is a good sound wine. The white Vöslauer is a good clean amber wine, and very sound. The sparkling Vöslauer will hold its own against any Champagne." Hungary is estimated to produce 96,000,000 gallons of wine—wine being the universal beverage of the nation—of which the best known is Tokay, as the wine of that particular district is called. Imperial Tokay is a very rich luscious wine, of peculiar flavour, and exquisite delicacy. It is very choice, extremely rare, and is much sought after. Of the old wine (vino vitrauno) it is said the Emperor of Austria, desiring to present some to the ex-King of Holland, and the stock in the imperial cellars not being considered sufficiently aged, two thousand bottles were obtained from Cracow, at seven ducats the bottle, which makes the cost about £3 6s. per bottle. This particular wine has been known to realize as much as £36 per dozen at Cracow, which is the principal depot for it. Why it is sold at so fabulous a price can only be accounted for by its extreme scarcity, the demand greatly exceeding the supply. There is some excellent wine produced in the neighbourhood of Tokay, and it has been estimated that the district can produce 4,000,000 bottles of wine, but of this quantity not more than one-fourth is Ausbruch. The wine of Buda (or Ofen) was once a great favourite in England. Next to Tokay in celebrity is Menos wine. It is red in colour, rich and highly flavoured. Another red wine, Carlowitz, is a sound wine. Of the white varieties, the Oedenburger is both a sound and refreshing wine. The dry Muscat, Szamarodi, and Erlauer, are also good wines for general use.

There are many other wines produced in different parts of Europe, which are principally consumed on the spot by the producers, and which, when they occasionally find their way to market, are mostly used for "blending" with wines of better and choicer growths. Of our Colonial wines, there are not any that can bear comparison with the wines of Europe.

The best Australia produces is a wine called *Cwarra*, which much resembles a second-rate Rhenish wine. Great efforts have, however, been made of late years to extend and improve the culture of the vine in this great country.

The Cape of Good Hope sends quantities of service-able wine to England; this is well known under the general term of Cape, or "South African;" but the best wine from that region is Constantia, so named from the township near where it is grown. Constantia is both red and white; it is a luscious wine, and has been held in high repute for more than a century. A red wine called Pontac, which is somewhat of a rough character, is much used in the colony.

America (where the vine is found growing wild) produces some good wine, but it is not very probable that much will find its way to this hemisphere. Their choicest production, Catawba, is thus eulogized by Longfellow:—

> "Very good in its way
> Is the Verzenay,
> Or the Sillery, soft and creamy;
> But Catawba wine
> Has a taste most divine,
> More dulcet, delicious, and dreamy."

It is a fact not generally known, that in the twelfth century vineyards were general in England. William of Malmesbury tells us that the wine made in the Vale of Gloucestershire not only was abundant, but little inferior to the wine of France: that this might have been possible has been proved by the experiments of late years of Sir Richard Worsley, in the last century, at St. Lawrence in the Isle of Wight, and by Mr. Hamilton, at Painshill. The last-named gentleman produced some wine fully equal to second-rate Champagne, but which, when kept for sixteen years, lost its Champagne characteristic, and became like dry Rhine wine, and gained strength; in fact, this gentleman affirms that it might have passed off for good Hock to anyone who was not a perfect connoisseur. The uncertainty of our climate, however, with its spring frosts and wet summers, and the expense of labour, in comparison with that- of other countries, would render vine-growing impossible.

The name of wine is familiarly bestowed on the fermented juice of all sub-acid fruits and other substances. The juice of the grape contains a considerable quantity of tartaric acid. This acid being but slightly soluble in wine, gradually settles on the sides of the bottle or cask, forming "the crust." Home-made wines—as those are termed which are made from various fruits—contain a very great proportion of citric or malic acid, which acids are soluble and dissolve in the liquor. In order to neutralize this acidity, it is requisite to add sugar, and also some spirit to prevent the fermentation the sugar would cause. This proceeding shows the difference which exists between wines made from the grape and those made from the gooseberry, &c. The brandy in foreign (or grape) wines, being in natural combination with the wine, which, blended with the colouring matter and other organic substances, produces on the digestive system an effect very different from that which follows the use of home-made wines, rendered strong by the addition, as shown, of brandy, which is much the same as spirits and water. Consequently, wine made from the grape is, from its nutritive properties, preferable to any other. Wine contains, moreover, a small quantity of a peculiar volatile principle, known as aenanthic ether, to which the vinous odour is due. It is not, however, correctly known to what cause the characteristic odour (or bouquet) is to be attributed which distinguishes one wine from another.

Bidding adieu to this subject, a few notes relative to the care of this generous beverage will not be out of place, for wine demands much care and attention, as well as the comfort of a good cellar.

In the first instance, it is desirable to keep the wine cellar at as even a temperature as possible; from 50° to 60° is a very safe one for most cellars. Where practicable, it will be found an excellent thing to have a jet or more of gas, which will be found to regulate both light and heat.

Each bin should be so built that a certain number of bottles will fit well in each tier (which might well contain just a dozen), without having occasion to use blocks. They present a better appearance, and stand less chance of disturbance. It will be desirable, for ready reference to quantity and date, &c, to have each bin labelled for this purpose. A slip of parchment is to be preferred to paper, which is apt to get damp.

If the cellar will admit of the accommodation, wine is best decanted there; the crust (or sediment) is thereby much less liable to be disturbed than by a longer move. The brilliancy and flavour, moreover, of the wine is frequently impaired by the agitation it undergoes during transit. Sometimes by that, or hasty and careless decanting, wine is often much injured, both in flavour and appearance, and the improvement, that it has perhaps taken years to effect, completely spoiled.

In decanting Port, always keep the chalk-mark upper-most, and use cambric in the strainer, so as to check the bees-wing, or second crust, which only forms some time after the first has formed; it is tarter, and freer from astringent matter than that deposited in the first crust. The other crust must on no account be allowed to pass. Other wines, especially Madeira, require great care in decanting. It is also desirable for the decanter to be quite as warm as the wine that enters it.

All sparkling wines should be binned in the coolest part of the cellar—the cork kept downward.

Sherries and other full-bodied wines are best decanted an hour or so before using; but Clarets, and other wines of that class, should be left undecanted till nearly when required for use.

When decanting in the cellar, you require a good light, also a cork bin, with pointed corkscrew, to prevent pieces of cork from getting into the wine; and a strainer, with some cambric, which should be hung up after use, or it will be apt to give a musty taste to the wine.

As regards bottling, it is strongly recommended that the merchant who supplied the wine should send an experienced cooper to do this. Many a good butt of wine has been entirely ruined by amateur bottling, and the blame thrown upon the wine-merchant. But if you have a small quantity, and wish to do it yourself, be particularly careful to have *clean*, *dry* bottles, and sound corks—it is a very bad economy to have inferior ones. You will also require a bottling-boot, apron, and cork-squeezer, a driving-mallet, which ought to weigh about a pound and a half, and a pan with a little, of the wine for dipping the corks in: take care to drive the corks in straight, and nearly home, leaving the space of about an inch between the wine and cork in the neck of the bottle. Be sure, ere you begin operations, that the wine is fine and brilliant, for, if bottled in a turbid state, it will not brighten afterwards. When bottled, bin as soon as you can, so that the wine may rest and cause the cork to swell. If your corks are too hard, put them in a vessel and pour on some boiling water; when swollen, strain and dry before using them.

Finings.—When isinglass is dissolved in diluted cold acetic acid (such as sour wine or beer), it immediately swells and assumes the appearance of jelly, which, although quite insoluble in cold, will readily mix with a good quantity of watery liquid. This is technically called finings, and is commonly used for fining-down any turbidity that may stubbornly remain. The action of the isinglass on the liquid seems to be purely mechanical, the gelatinous matter slowly subsiding to the bottom of the cask, and carrying with it the insoluble substance which caused the turbidity.

To fine White Wines.—Dissolve one ounce of isinglass in a pint of boiling liquor, which, when cold, forms a kind of jelly; whisk up some of this jelly into a froth with a little of the wine intended to be fined, then stir it up well amongst the wine in the cask, and bung up tight. By this means the wine will be bright and fine in ten or twelve days.

To fine Red Wines.—Take the whites of fifteen or twenty eggs for a pipe of wine, beat these up into a froth, and mix in the same manner as for the white wines. There are other modes of fining, but these are best understood by the wine-merchant; in fact, when wine requires fining, it is always better to entrust the operation to some experienced cooper or cellarman.

ALCOHOL

Alcohol, which is the living characteristic, or principle of wines, spirits, beer, and all intoxicating liquors, is produced from numerous sources; all vegetables containing farina or saccharine matter can be employed to obtain alcohol. The various peculiarity of flavour, &c, in the different spirits, is owing to some alien substance, as an essential oil, and other causes; for the basis is the same, from whatever source derived.

Absolute, or pure, Alcohol, is a limpid, colourless fluid, of agreeable smell; it readily absorbs water, and unless it be carefully protected, it soon loses its purity: pure alcohol never freezes.

Proof Spirit is a term used when spirit is proved of the proper strength; that is when it is found to contain two pints of rectified spirits of wine with one of distilled water.

Rectified Spirit and *Spirits of Wine* are synonymous terms.

The origin of the discovery of alcohol is unknown. Its name, "alcohol" seems to give the Arabs the claim of being the inventors of the art of distillation; at all events, the art was known at an early period in Spain and Italy, having been introduced into Spain by the Moors. It was first used as a medicine, and was then distilled from the grape. The Genoese afterwards distilled it from grain, and called it *aqua vitae, i.e.,* water of life. Alcohol comprises, under its designation, the following principal varieties: spirits of wine, brandy, rum, arrack, gin, whisky, &c. As spirits of wine, it is much used for pharmaceutical and other purposes. Its specific gravity is fixed by the London Pharmacopoeia at 9.20.

Brandy.—Derived from the German word *Brantwein,* i.e. wine that has undergone the action of fire, is an ardent spirit, used more generally than any other. It was first made in Sicily, at the commencement of the fourteenth century, and is the spirit most commonly produced in wine countries; that we obtain from France being the most highly esteemed. The department of Charente produces the most famous and choice Brandies of France, known by the name Cognac, Jernac, Champagne, &c.: the best is made from the grape named *folle blanche,* which only yields a poor white wine. In good years, this wine will produce a fifth of spirit at 22° to 23°, but in bad years, nine or ten parts of wine are required to produce one of Brandy. The Brandy distilled from the red grape is inferior to the *folle blanche,* and does not possess the bouquet of genuine Cognac. Cognac Brandy, as the Brandy of the Charente is called, owes its excellence to the care exercised in fermenting the wine, that it be not impregnated with an acrid oil which is contained in the skin of the grape, a drop of which would suffice to deteriorate a large quantity of good Brandy spirit. It is this oil that renders *eau, de vie de marc* (or Brandy distilled from the lees and refuse of the grape, after wine-making) so unpleasantly coarse and unpleasant in flavour. The wine-growers in the Brandy districts of Charente carry on the distillation themselves, nearly each vine-land being furnished with stills and the necessary apparatus, and the utmost pains are taken to make the Brandy of the greatest degree of purity. From whatever vine it is obtained, it is at first perfectly colourless or white Brandy. The best produce of the still is known as *eau de vie première*, and is remarkable for its delicate rich bouquet and flavour, rendering it pre-eminent above all brandies: this quality, when kept in casks, assumes a pale amber colour. The second distillation, or common Brandy, is an inferior produce, being rarely exported: it is known as *eau de vie ordinaire*; it is made from spoilt or inferior red or white wines, and constitutes the French Brandy in ordinary use.

Eau de vie d'Aisne is synonymous with *eau de vie de marc*, the inferior spirit already noticed.

Eau de vie d'Andaye, is remarkable for its peculiar fennel-like odour; it is a choice and excellent Brandy, and often imitated by mixing a quart of good old Cognac with ¼ gill distilled aniseed water, and ¾ gill of clear syrup. A few fennel seeds, steeped in ordinary Brandy, is called *eau de vie de Rhé*. The Brandies of Rochelle, Bordeaux, Languedoc, and others, are good French Brandies, which are superior to the Brandies of Italy, Spain, and other countries: every soil, climate, and grape varies, as regards quality of yield of Brandy.

Foreign Brandy is generally overproof. A great *desideratum* among distillers in this country is to imitate foreign spirits, such as Brandy, Rum, Geneva, &c., and they succeed to a tolerable degree of perfection. English spirits, judiciously managed, can be made to resemble foreign (grape) Brandy very successfully, the best being made with clean malt spirit, mixed with ordinary Brandy, then brought up to the desired flavour with Raisin Brandy or some other spirit. Good British, or Patent, Brandy is much to be preferred to many of the foreign spirits, improperly called Brandy, but which are distilled from the beet, carrot, potato, &c, and are brought up to the desired flavour by various ingredients. Guernsey Brandy is made from beetroot spirit; Dantzic Brandy from rye, mixed with the roots of the *Calamus aromaticus*; Cider Brandy is made from the residuum of apples and pears, after the cider or perry has been drawn off; Peach Brandy, so well-known and appreciated in the United States, is obtained from peaches, by fermentation and distillation. The New Jersey Peach Brandy is esteemed the best: an imitation of this brandy will be furnished at the end of this article. *Whisky*, which may justly claim to be considered as the national spirit of the Irish and Scotch, is obtained from the fermented wort of malt and grain; it agrees in most of its properties with Gin, but is lighter and more stomachic; it is stronger than Gin, and is undoubtedly also the best spirit for general use. The Whisky distilled from malt is esteemed the best. The inferior Whiskies are obtained from oats, rye, potatoes, barley, &c. The peculiar smoky flavour is imparted by the wash being purposely left to burn a little. An imitation Whisky is made by adding a few drops of purified fusel-oil and creosote to clean spirit, or gin. Of the true *Potheen*, Professor Donovan, who was present at a genuine Irish illicit Potheen distillation, says, "that he is doubtful whether the turf used is the cause of the flavour of the spirit, but attributes this to the grains and mode of distillation. The barley is wetted with bog-water, in order to excite germination, the malt dried with turf, instead of coal. The malt then is mixed with about one-fourth of raw corn, and the mashing is made in a kind of vat, the bottom of which is covered with young heath and oat husks—to supply the place of a false one; when the wash begins to boil in the still, the fire is suddenly quenched, and the spirit which runs, though weak, is of true flavour. The singlings are distilled again, and yield the true Potheen."

Gin.—This well-known compound corn-spirit derives its name from the French word *genièvre*, or juniper. This spirit is very popular in many parts of Europe, especially amongst the Swiss, Dutch, and our own country. Dutch Gin (*Hollands*) is very different from the English Gin; it is a rich, mellow, soft spirit; its peculiar flavour is due to its being flavoured with juniper: the best comes from Schiedam and Rotterdam. English Gin varies considerably in point of flavour; Plymouth Gin closely resembles Hollands. Almost every distiller or rectifier has a mode of his own in making Gin, and in giving it his own characteristic flavour with the aid of oil of turpentine or other aromatics.

Rum, a well-known spirit, chiefly made in the West Indies, is obtained from the distillation of the fermented skimmings of the sugar-boilers, with the strainings and washings of the sugar-works, adding some crude cane-juice, necessary to impart the flavour. Good Rum is of a clear light brown colour, and of mellow and soft taste; when obtained pure it can be depended on as a very wholesome spirit, but if impure, it is most injurious; when rectified to a strength nearly equal to spirits of wine, it is called Double-distilled Rum. The best comes from Jamaica; that from the Leeward Islands is an inferior quality. The custom of putting slices of pine-apple in the puncheon originated the term "Pine-apple Rum." It is the favourite liquor in the West Indies and North America, and the regulation spirit of the British Navy.

Arrack is the name given to all the spirits made in the East. That distilled from a juice which flows from the cocoa-nut-tree, and called toddy, is the best; the arrack made from rice and other substances is very inferior. Arrack is a clear spirit, and, when well aged, is peculiarly good; it can be further improved, and made like a liqueur, by adding some slices of pine-apple. That which comes from Java is the best: the Chinese also produce an arrack, which, when old, fully equals any other. Tungusian arrack is a spirituous liquor made by the Tartars of Tungusia, of sour mares' milk, fermented, and distilled twice or thrice, between two earthen vessels closely stopped; the liquor escaping through in a small wooden pipe.

Gentian Spirit is much used by the Swiss mountaineers; it is a bitter spirit, made from gentian root. Of the other varieties of alcoholic liquors, very few are known beyond the spots where they are distilled.

There are various alcoholic productions which, although ranking as liqueurs or cordials, are dangerously strong and seductive; such as Kirschwasser, Maraschino, Goldwasser, Noyeau, and many others, of which a description will be given. The difference between Kirschwasser (cherry-water) and Maraschino (both being spirits distilled from the cherry, which fruit is remarkable for the variety of favourite beverages it produces) is this: Kirsch is distilled from bruised cherries, and is a pure spirit, while Maraschino is distilled from the pulp of the cherries, mixed with honey: honey is also added to the spirit after distillation. The best Maraschino (de Zara) is made from the Marasca cherry, which grows very plentifully in Dalmatia and Northern Italy. The choicest is made in or near the town of Zara, in Dalmatia. Fictitious Maraschino is made by sweetening and flavouring Kirschwasser.

Kirschwasser is a common and favourite liquor with the Swiss and Germans. When this spirit is of good age, it is much pleasanter to the taste than when new. It has the reputation of assisting digestion, and has the curious property of decomposing fruit when added to it in bottle.

Goldwasser (which derives its name from portions of gold leaf floating in the liqueur) is a spirit made principally in Dantzic, and is rectified with cinnamon, aniseed, and other aromatics.

Kümmel is the favourite liqueur of Russia; the best is made at Weissenchein, in Esthonia; that made at Riga is also very good.

Chartreuse, a pleasant stomachic liqueur, is made by the Monks of the Grand Chartreuse, near Grenoble. There are as many as four varieties of this liqueur: a pure spirit, which is of a clear light green, and the bottle is incased in a turned wooden case; a light green, which is sweet and strong; an amber, which is not so sweet; and the white sort.

The well-known liqueur *Noyeau*, of which the best comes from Martinique, requires good age, and being much sought after, is both scarce and expensive.

Curaçoa, Cherry Brandy, and other compound liqueurs, are mostly importations from Holland and Denmark. The delicious Copenhagen Cherry Brandy, of which Heering's is the finest quality, is made from the small black wild cherries so plentiful in Norway. No imitation can equal the *bona fide* old Dutch Curaçoa. These liqueurs and other exquisite concoctions are well-known to the connoisseur, who, as he passes the ambrosial fluid over his tongue (knowing that such delicious conceptions should be sipped, *not bolted*), fully appreciates the exquisite pleasure his palate experiences as each peculiar and delicate flavour is brought out.

For general purposes, the use of liqueurs is much abridged by reason of their excessive cost; yet there are very many that can be successfully imitated, and become, by judicious treatment and age, equal to the elaborate foreign production, at about one-third or less of the cost.

In making liqueurs, it is highly important to employ the very best materials, and to observe great cleanliness and care in manipulation. The French *liquoristes*, who stand pre-eminent for their delicious cordials, only employ the best materials: they also distinguish three qualities of compounds, viz., *Ratafias*, or simple liqueurs, as Noyeau, Anisette Water, &c, in which the spirit, sugar, and aromatic are in minute quantities; the *Cremes*, or such choice liqueurs as Maraschino, Dantzic, Goldwater, &c.; the oils, *Huíles*, or fine liqueurs, containing a more syrupy consistence, as Curaçoa, Anisette, Bordeaux, &c.

There are two modes of making liqueurs, viz., by infusion and distillation. Most of them can be made by careful and judicious infusion, quite as well as by the tedious process of distillation, for it is only when some objectionable flavour is present, in the form of an essential oil, that distillation is positively necessary.

In making liqueurs, it is quite requisite to use great care and cleanliness throughout the operation, and to employ only the best materials, the principal being clean spirit, distilled water, and pure white sugar. The neglect of either of these will result in failure to produce a good liqueur. The next, and a most important essential, is to guard against using too much flavouring matter, or the injudicious combination of discordant flavours—the inexperienced *liquoriste* being apt to underrate the power of some of the aromatics or essential oils. It is hence better to use a little less than more, for the want can easily be supplied by the addition of any extra flavour required. If the compound is cloudy, do not use water, but a little spirit; or clarify it. Never use any other (except given) than pure rectified spirits of wine. Gin, above all, should be avoided, on account of its pervading flavour. If the spirits of wine is too strong, reduce to the strength desired with filtered soft water. Treble-refined sugar should always be used. In making syrup for liqueurs, use one pound of sugar to one pint of water, brought to the boil, skimmed, and, when cool, add a very little spirit. Never add the spirit while the liquor is hot. Only use the outer peel of any of the citrous order (the white pith being worse than useless). The best mode to obtain the ambrosial essence of oranges, lemons, &c, is to rub the outer rind (free from specs) with a piece of sugar, scraping the essence from the lump as it requires: this sugared essence constitutes the oleo-saccharum of liquorists and confectioners.

In some liqueurs the aromatics should be mixed first with the syrup; in others, the sugar dissolved in an infusion of flavoury substances; and, in others, the flavoury substance should be mixed with the spirit.

Maceration is the immersion of any substance in spirit or any other liquid, for a certain time. To properly macerate, the liquid should be just warm, of a blood heat.

A Decoction is simply the boiling of the ingredients in a vessel of water, set in a saucepan, filled with boiling water (*bain-marie*), the lid being occasionally raised.

SYRUPS AND LIQUEURS

Capillaire (proper) is made by infusing 2 oz. of the maiden-hair fern (*Adiantum capillus Veneris*) in 1 ½ pint of boiling water, and 2 lbs. of loaf sugar, which pour while boiling hot on 2 oz. more of the fern; in ten hours strain clear.

To Clarify Syrups.—Beat up the syrup cold with white of egg; heat; remove scum when clear; while hot strain.

For Filtering.—Use tammy or other proper substance; if paper is required, the best Russian is preferable to any other.

To Colour.—For green, use parsley or spinach leaves, digested in spirit; for violet, mix blue and red together; for green, mix blue and yellow; for red, use cochineal or Brazil wood; for blue, use indigo or Prussian blue; for yellow, fawn, or amber, use tincture of saffron, or caramel (burnt sugar).

Sugar.—This useful substance is found more or less in most vegetable substances. It is extracted most readily from the juice of the sugar-cane (*Saccharum officinorum*); and also from the sugar-maple (*Acer saccharum*); in France and other parts, from the beetroot; in China, from the sweet sorgho (*Sorghum saccharum*); and in other countries, from various sources. The sugar used in this country is the cane-sugar. To make which the canes are crushed, the juice collected, then slowly heated to nearly boiling point; a little hydrate of lime is added, which clears it; it is then skimmed, and subjected to a great heat, till sufficiently concentrated by rapid evaporation; it is then cooled in shallow open pans, and put into casks with holes bored in to allow the un-crystallizable portion (*molasses*) to drain away: this is the common treacle of our shops. What remains in the cask is what we know as raw sugar, called, in commerce, Muscovado.

Lump Sugar.—To make lump (or loaf) sugar, raw sugar is first redissolved in water, some albumen added, and, if required, a little lime-water; it is then boiled, skimmed, and clarified by being filtered through animal charcoal; then subjected to a great heat, and when at the proper degree of syrup, is poured into conical moulds, where it drains,* dries, and becomes solid, and soon forms ordinary loaf-sugar. When the crystallization takes place slowly, it forms into sugar-candy, which is coloured as required.

Barley-sugar is made by subjecting loaf-sugar to the requisite heat, and then letting it cool.

Good sugar ought to feel dry to the touch, and have a sparkling appearance when broken; it should be close

---

* This thicker draining (or syrup) is known in shops as "golden syrup."

in texture, and hard to break. It requires for its solution one-third of its weight in cold, and less of boiling, water.

To make Syrup and Clarify.—Beat up the white of one egg into a froth, which well mix with 3 lbs. of sugar, diluted with 3 pints of water. Put the mixture into a pan over a steady stove fire, having a little cold water at hand to prevent the syrup boiling over. Let the sugar rise three times, each time checking the boiling over by a little cold water; the fourth time completely skim, and so continue till all the froth is cleared off. Strain through a flannel or hair bag. This syrup will be found sufficient for all the ordinary requirements of making liqueurs and similar purposes. It is noteworthy to add, that it will be found best to employ only the best refined sugar, and filtered water, soft if procurable; by so doing it often saves the trouble of clarification, which invariably becomes necessary when inferior ingredients are used. The proportion of 30 parts of sugar to 16 parts of water also makes an excellent syrup.

In preparing syrups employ as little heat as possible. The best plan is to pour the water cold over the sugar, and let it slowly melt; and, when well saturated, bring it up to the boil by a gentle heat, and then keep simmering to the point desired. If a syrup is bottled while at boiling heat, and immediately corked and tied down with bladder, it will last a long time in a perfect state. Syrups are best kept in a cool temperature.

To make Orgeat, or Syrup of Almonds.—Take 1 lb. of sweet and 1 oz. of bitter almonds; blanch them; beat in a marble mortar to a smooth paste; add juice of half a lemon and a pint of barley-water; pass this through a sieve. Again, with a little of the liquid beat up the residue of the almonds till every particle is thoroughly mixed with the liquid; add another pint of barley-water; strain clear, and to every pint of liquid add 1 ¼ lb. of sugar and 1 drachm of orange-flower water and rectified spirit.

Mock Arrack, or Vauxhall Nectar.—To 1 quart of pure (uncoloured) Jamaica rum, add ½ drachm of flowers of benzoin, ½ fluid drachm essence of pine-apple; digest, and keep agitating for a month; then add 1 gill of skimmed milk; agitate well; in a week bottle off the clear portion. This is an excellent liqueur, and very useful for Punches à la Romaine or other kinds.

Another Mode.—Dissolve 1 scruple of flowers of benzoin in 1 quart of good rum; add a sliced pine-apple, or ½ fluid drachm of essence of pine-apple, and 4 grains balsam of Tolu; digest three weeks; add a gill of skimmed milk ; agitate well.

Aniseed.—Drop on a lump of sugar 3 drops of oil of aniseed, 1 drop each of oil of cinnamon and carraway; dissolve in a pint of spirit; when well digested, add 1 pint of clarified syrup.

Anisette de Bordeaux is a liqueur made by distilling fennel, anise and coriander seeds, which are added to brandy and syrup. It can thus be imitated: take of oil of aniseed 7 drops, of oil of cinnamon 3 drops, oil of carraway 2 drops, dropped on a lump of sugar, which infuse in 1 ½ pint of rectified spirit, adding ½ drachm sweet fennel seeds; in two days strain clear; add 1 pint clarified syrup.

Amour sans fin.—Take 6 drops otto of roses, 13 drops oil of neroli, 13 drops oil of cloves; dissolve in a quart of pure spirits of wine, and while dissolving assist the process by agitating the liquor; then filter clear ; add this to 7 pints of clear syrup, and colour with cochineal.

Cherry Brandy, No. 1.—Bruise 3 lbs. of black cherries (wild ones preferable), cracking the stones; put the mass into a jar, with a few young cherry leaves; add 3 pints of brandy, or pure spirit; in three months strain off; add 2 lbs. of clear sugar, after which it will be ready for use in a week.

Cherry Brandy, No. 2.—Into a stewpan put 8 lbs. of clean picked cherries, viz., 7 lbs. of black and 1 lb. of red; let this stand on a hot plate, taking the precaution not to let the juice burn; when well done, strain off the juice through a bag, add 1 lb. of sugar to every 3 lbs. of juice; give the juice and sugar a boil up; when cool, add equal quantities of brandy and juice.

Cherry Brandy, No. 3.—To each pint of brandy add 1 lb. of Morello cherries, ½ pint of the expressed juice of small black cherries, 3 bruised bitter almonds, 1 lb. of bruised sugar-candy; will be ready for use in two months.

Cherry Brandy, No. 4 (*a la Hall*).—Take 10 lbs. Morello cherries, 10 lbs. wild cherries, 2 lbs. strawberries, 2 lbs. raspberries, 8 pints of brandy, 4 oz. of sugar to every pint of juice. Bruise the cherries and stones together in a mortar, smashing the stones; add the rest of the fruit, which bruise also; then 2 drachms of coriander seeds and 1 drachm of mace; mix all the ingredients together well; macerate for one month, in a covered jar. It may require more sugar, but that will depend on the ripeness of the fruit; if too acid, add 2 oz. more sugar to every pint of liquor; then strain clear and bottle.

Carraway Brandy.—Steep 1 oz. of carraway seeds (bruised) in 1 pint of brandy; in one week strain; add 6 oz. of loaf sugar.

Currant, Black, or Red Brandy.—Take 1 quart of black or red currants, and fill up with brandy; in two months strain; add sugar to taste.

Ginger Brandy.—Bruise 1 oz. of ginger; add 1 bottle of brandy; strain; add syrup.

Juniper Brandy.—Dissolve ½ drachm oil of juniper in 1 quart of pure spirit (or brandy); add ½ lb. of sugar dissolved in 1 quart of water.

Lemon Brandy.—Steep the thin peels of 6 lemons and 2 bitter almonds in 1 quart of brandy; macerate two weeks; strain with pressure, adding ½ pint of water and 1 lb. of loaf-sugar.

Lemon Brandy.—Take peels of 4 lemons, 1 bitter almond, bottle of brandy; strain; add juice of 2 lemons, and ½ lb of loaf-sugar.

Orange Brandy.—Dissolve in ½ gallon of brandy, 1 drachm oil of orange, and 1 drop oil of neroli, adding 1 lb. of sugar.

Orange Brandy.—Into a large jar, put 6 Seville and 2 Tangerine oranges; cover them with brandy; in three months' time, strain off the brandy, sweeten to taste, and cover the oranges over with syrup—they will make an excellent sweetmeat.

Cassis.—Infuse for one week in 1 quart of brandy ¼ oz. of cinnamon and 2 cloves (bruised); then add 1 pint of black currants; let these macerate for two months; strain with pressure; add ½ lb. of sugar to every pint; bottle for use.

Cinnamon Cordial.—Let ¼ lb. Ceylon cinnamon (bruised)

be infused in 1 quart of brandy for ten days; then add 1
drop essence of orange-peel and cardamoms; colour dark
brown with caramel.

Cassia Cordial.—In 1 pint of spirits of wine infuse 3 drops
of oil of cassia and 2 drops oil of lemon-peel.

Cedrat.—Dissolve 30 drops oil of cedrat in 1 pint of pure
spirits of wine; add, when dissolved, 1 pint of syrup.

Creme de Citron.—Dissolve 30 drops oil of citron in 1 pint
of spirits of wine; colour with 2 drops tincture of saffron;
add 1 quart of syrup.

Creme de Cannelle.—Dissolve 10 drops oil of cinnamon and
2 of oil of roses in 1 pint of rectified spirit; when well
digested add 1 quart of syrup, and colour with cochineal.

Creme de Barbadoes.—Put the juice and thin peel of 3
lemons and 1 citron, in a jar with 1 quart of spirits of
wine and 3 oz. fresh-chopped balm leaves; macerate for
one month; strain with pressure; add a syrup of 2 lbs. of
sugar, and 1 quart of water; a drop or two of lemon-grass
oil in the spirit is a grateful addition.

Creme de Menth.—Dissolve in ½ pint of spirits of wine 1 drop
oil of citron, 6 drops oil of mint; colour green by a mixture
of saffron and indigo; add 1 pint of syrup.

Creme de Menth.—Macerate for 24 hours, in 1 quart of spirit,
1 lb. of spearmint, and the thin rinds of 4 lemons; strain
clear, add water and sugar 1 gallon.

Creme de Nymphe.—Take 9 drops oil of cinnamon, 5 drops oil
of mace, 3 drops oil of roses; dissolve in 5 pints of pure
spirits of wine; add 5 lbs. of sugar and 1 quart of water,
near the boiling point.

Creme de Cedrat with Champagne.—Dissolve ¼ oz. oil of

cedrat in ½ gallon of alcohol; add 1 bottle of champagne and 13 lbs. of sugar dissolved in 1 gallon of water.

Creme de Naphe.—1 pint of orange-flower water, 2 lbs. pure refined sugar, dissolved in 2 quarts of spirits.

Creme de Cacao.—Infuse 1 lb. best Caraccas cocoa-nibs, crushed, in 3 quarts of brandy; add 1 oz. of vanilla; digest a fortnight; strain; add 3 quarts of weak syrup.

Creme de Noyeau.—Digest ½ oz. blanched and crushed bitter almonds in ¼ pint of pure spirit; in two days, add 1 gill of filtered soft water, 3 oz. of sugar, 1 drop essence of cochineal.

Creme de Noyeau.—Of peach kernels, blanched and bruised, 1 oz.; proof spirit, 1 pint; cinnamon, ¼ oz.; macerate two weeks; strain with pressure; add 10 oz. of syrup and ¼ pint orange-flower water.

Creme de Noyeau de Martinique.—Take 5 oz. bitter almonds, blanched in cold water, and then bruised; digest them in 3 quarts spirits of wine; add 30 drops essence of lemon; in a fortnight, strain with pressure; add a syrup made of 6 lbs. of loaf-sugar, 1 gallon of water, and 1 pint of orange-flower water.

Creme d'Orange.—Take 3 mandarin oranges steeped in 1 pint of pure spirit; strain in one month (with pressure); add 1 drop of neroli and 1 quart of syrup.

Creme d'Orange with Champagne.—Take 1 drachm oil of orange dissolved in ½ gallon of spirit; add bottle of champagne and 1 gallon of good syrup.

Creme de Rose.—Add to 1 pint of spirits 8 drops oil of roses, 1 drop oil of nutmeg, 1 drop oil of cinnamon, 1 quart of good syrup; colour with cochineal to a bright red.

Creme de Vanille.—Flavour sweetened spirit, containing the proportion of 3 ½ lbs. of sugar per gallon, with vanilla bean according to strength desired.

Creme de Vanille.—Into 1 pint of spirits of wine put 7 drops tincture of vanilla; when well digested, add 1 quart of thin syrup; filter clear.

Delight of the Mandarins.—To 1 drachm aniseed add seeds of musk, or ambrette, 2 drachms, safflower ½ drachm, cinnamon ¼ drachm; bruise these ingredients well together; digest in 1 quart pure spirits of wine; strain in ten days, and add 1 quart of syrup (weak, 60 u.p.).

Curaçao.—Into 1 quart of boiling water dissolve 1 lb. of sugar-candy; boil up the syrup, *clarify*, and cool; digest 120 drops (2 fluid drachms) of oil of bitter orange in 1 ½ pint of pure rectified spirit, which add to the syrup; colour with caramel.

Curaçao.—Take 24 Seville oranges, not pricked or broken; put these into a jar, cover with good brown brandy; digest for a month; strain; to every quart add 1 lb. of sugar-candy; digest another week; strain clear. An excellent Curaçao; the fruit can be used as a sweet by being placed in syrup.

Curaçao d'Holland.—Soak in soft distilled water 1 lb. Curaçao orange-peel, ¼ lb. Ceylon cinnamon; add the strained juice of 16 oranges; boil for five minutes; add 4 gallons plain white syrup, and, when cool, 2 ½ gallons of brandy, or pure spirit; digest two weeks ; filter clear; colour with tincture of saffron.

Citronelle.—Take essence of orange, 1 drachm; essence of lemon, 1 ½ drachm; oil of cloves, 6 drops; oil of cinnamon, 12 drops; oil of coriander, 15 drops. Infuse in pure spirits of wine 5 pints well digested, add 1 quart distilled water; filter clear; sweeten with clarified sugar, q.s.

Citronelle.—Take 4 fresh lemons, 3 drops of lemon-grass oil, 2 drops of essence of cinnamon, 1 drop of oil of coriander; digest two weeks in 1 quart of spirit; then add 3 pints clarified weak syrup; in two weeks strain clear.

Eau d'Argent.—1 drachm of oil of cedrats, 3 drachms oil of roses, dissolved in three quarts of rectified spirit; when well digested, add a clarified syrup of 2 ½ lbs. of sugar in 1 ½ gallon of water; filter and bottle; mix previously 10 sheets of silverfoil, cut in small pieces.

Eau de Chasseurs.—To 15 drops oil of peppermint, 4 drops of oil of mace, dissolved in 1 quart of pure spirit; add a clarified syrup of 1 lb. of loaf-sugar to 2 quarts of water.

Eau de Fleurs d'Oranges.—To 17 drops of neroli dissolved, by well agitating in 1 quart of spirit, add a clarified syrup of 1 lb. of sugar, in 3 quarts of water.

Eau de Belles Dames.—Take 16 drops of essence of vanilla, 1 drop of oil of roses, 2 drops of oil of neroli; dissolve in 3 pints of proof spirit; add a clarified syrup of 2 ½ lbs. of sugar to 3 quarts of water.

Eau de Thé.—To ½ lb. of hyson add ¼ lb. of souchong tea; macerate for ten days in 1 gallon of alcohol; strain with pressure; add clarified syrup, 2 ½ gallons.

Eau de Thé.—Make an infusion with 1 quart of boiling water of ½ oz. gunpowder tea, ¼ oz. orange pekoe, ¼ oz. black tea; strain clear; add equal quantities of pure spirit, syrup and water, with a teaspoonful orange-flower water; colour green.

Elixir de Violettes.—To 1 pint of syrup of violets, ½ pint syrup of raspberries, add 1 quart of pure spirit; mix, colour with blue and red, for violet.

Elephant's Milk.—To 1 oz. of benzoin gum, dissolved in 1 pint of spirits of wine, add 1 lb. of sugar, dissolved in 1 quart of boiling water.

Goldwasser.—Dissolve in 1 pint of clean spirit 1 drachm of mace, 2 drops oil of cinnamon, 3 drops oil of citron, 6 drops of aniseed, 2 drops of oil of roses; in one week strain with pressure; filter; clear; add equal quantity of clear syrup, and a few leaves of gold leaf.

Ginger Gin.—Infuse 2 oz. candied orange-peel and 2 oz. bruised ginger in 2 pints of gin; add 1 lb. loaf-sugar.

Gin and Tansey.—Put some tansey in a bottle; fill up with gin.

Gin and Wormwood.—Use wormwood instead of tansey.

Gin and Sherry.—Use cherries and sherry, with gin.

Gingerette.—Infuse in 1 pint of pure spirit (gin or whisky) 3 oz. of bruised ginger; strain with pressure; add 1 ½ lbs. of sugar, and 2 ½ drachms of citric acid; dissolve in 3 pints of water.

Huile de Thé.—With 1 pint of water make an infusion of 1 ½ oz. of green tea; strain with pressure; add a clarified syrup of 4 lbs. of sugar to 1 quart of water, 1 pint of spirits of wine, and a tablespoonful syrup of roses or violets.

Juniper Ratafia.—To 4 oz. of juniper berries, 1 oz. of cinnamon, ¼ oz. cloves, add 10 grains of coriander and aniseeds; thoroughly bruise the spices together, also the berries, and well mix; add 1 quart of spirits of wine, ½ pint of syrup; keep closely stopped for six weeks; add ½ pint of water; in two days strain, clear, and bottle.

Kümmel.—To 1 pint of pure spirit add 50 drops oil of carraway and 1 pint of syrup.

Kirschwasser.—Macerate in 1 pint of spirit 2 lbs. of bruised cherry-stones, and 1 dozen grey cherry leaves (bruised), and strain; 1 pint of Kentish cherry-juice is sometimes added.

Life of Man.—12 drops oil of lemon, 9 drops oil of cloves, 3 drops oil of mace; dissolve in 1 quart of alcohol; add 2 ½ lbs. of sugar, dissolved in 5 pints of water; strain; clear; add 2 drops essence of cochineal.

Liqueur de Quatre Fruits.—Take 2 lbs. of strawberries, 1 lb. raspberries, 1 lb. red currants, and 2 lbs. of Morella cherries, and 1 dozen apricot kernels (as they ripen); extract the clear juice, sweeten with white sugar-candy (pounded)—be sure not to make it like a syrup—then strain clear; to every pint of juice add ¼ pint of pale brandy; bottle for use.

Liqueur de Thé, à la Russe.—To 1 pint of strong green tea (clear) add ½ pint of lemon-juice (strained), ½ pint of pure rectified spirit, 1 quart of capillaire, and 2 drops essence of orange or lemon peel.

Liqueur de Thé.—Make a syrup of 2 ½ lbs. of sugar to 2 quarts of water; when clear, add 1 oz. hyson tea, and ¼ oz. cowslip hyson; gently heat, and, when nearly cool, strain with pressure; add 1 quart of pure spirit, or Scotch whisky, and 2 or 3 drops tincture of saffron, or green colouring.

Liquodilla.—Thin peel of 4 sweet oranges and 2 lemons, in 1 pint of brandy or rum; macerate a fortnight; strain with pressure; add the juice of the fruit, also 1 quart of clarified syrup.

Lovage.—To 1 gallon of gin, mixed with 1 pint clear syrup, add a tincture made by macerating 1 lb. of fresh-cut celery roots and 1 oz. of sweet fennel in pure spirit for two days; strain by pressure; add 1 drachm of oil of cinnamon, 30 drops oil of carraway seeds, well flavoured, and strain clear.

Liqueur d'Henri.—Of aniseed use 60 drops; oil of angelica, 15 drops; oil of cassia, 10 drops; oil of carraway, 8 drops; proof spirit, ½ gallon; keep closely corked.

Imperial Nectar.—Infuse in 1 pint spirits of wine 1 oz. of bruised blanched apricot or peach kernels; 1 scruple oil of orange, ½ grated nutmeg, 2 drachms oil of cinnamon, 1 drop oil of cloves; add 1 quart of raisin wine, ¼ pint caramel; put these ingredients into a stone bottle for a month or longer; add 2 drops essence of lemon; after this has been in another fortnight, filter clear; add 4 pints boiling milk; filter and bottle.

Noyeau, No. 1.—Macerate ½ lb. French plums, bruised to a pulp; add the thin peel rind of 1 Seville or 2 sweet oranges, &c., 1 oz. sweet almonds bruised in a covered vessel, and pour in 1 quart of spirits of wine for one month; strain, with pressure; add 1 drop oil of cinnamon, and 2 ½ pints of weak syrup; colour with a little saffron.

Noyeau, No. 2.—Take 1 lb. of peaches, 1 lb. of apricots sliced, and the stones well smashed; put the fruit into a jar, with 1 lb. of good loaf-sugar; add peeling of 1 orange; pour on 1 pint of water just off the boil; cover; digest the stones in 1 quart of spirits of wine for four days, which add to the fruit, &c.; in a week strain clear, by pressure.

Noyeau Spirit, No. 3.—Take of gin or whisky, 1 pint; sugar,

¼ lb.; mix, and flavour carefully with essence of bitter almonds, to taste.

Noyeau, No. 4.—Bruise 1 lb. of cherry or plum stones; add 1 pint of spirit and 1 drachm of bruised ginger and cinnamon; digest one week; strain; add 1 fluid drachm orange-flower water, and 1 pint weak syrup.

Noyeau, No. 5.—Take 5 drops essence of bitter almonds, 2 drops oil of orange; digest in ½ pint spirits of wine; add 1 pint of clear syrup; filter clear.

Noyeau Ratafia.—½ lb. apricot kernels blanched in cold water, well bruised; macerate six weeks in 1 quart of spirits of wine; strain with pressure; add 2 ½ lbs. of sugar, dissolved in 3 pints of water.

Orange Nectar.—To ½ drachm oil of neroli, add 2 ½ oz. of thin orange-peel; macerate for ten days in 2 ½ pints of alcohol; strain with expression; add a syrup, made of 2 ½ lbs. of sugar to a gallon of water; colour yellow with saffron.

Persico.—Fill up a bottle with good, clear, young peach leaves; pour in as much as possible of good brandy; in six weeks strain; sweeten with syrup; bottle for use.

Peppermint.—Spirits of wine 2 oz., English oil of peppermint ¼ oz.; add a few drops on sugar when required.

Parfait Amour.—Infuse in 1 pint of spirits of wine ¼ teaspoonful of vanilla powder; add the oleo-saccharum of 2 lemons and 1 lb. of sugar; colour with cochineal.

Ratafia d'Angelique.—Take 5 oz. fresh-cut angelica root, and 2 oz. bruised juniper berries; macerate ten days in 1 gallon of pure rectified spirit; add a syrup made of 5 lbs. of sugar to 1 gallon of water; strain with pressure and clear; colour light green with a mixture of indigo and saffron.

Ratafia d'Abricots.—Boil 1 lb. of apricots with 1 ½ lb. of sugar and 1 ½ quarts of water for ten minutes; when cool, add 1 pint of alcohol; digest two days; filter clear.

Ratafia de Framboises.—1 lb. of raspberries, boiled for a quarter of an hour, with ½ pint of water and 2 lbs. of sugar; dissolve in 3 pints of water; add 1 quart of brandy.

Ratafia de Groseilles.—Take 1 lb. of red currants, ½ of white, well strained; the juice boiled five minutes with 2 ½ lbs. of sugar, and dissolved in 3 ½ pints of water; when cool, add 1 quart of spirit; filter clear.

Quince Liqueur.—Bruise 12 cloves and 3 oz. bitter almonds, and ¼ lb. coriander seeds, which digest in 2 quarts of cognac; when well flavoured, strain; make 1 quart of quince-juice, 2 lbs. of sugar, 2 drops essence of apple; when fit, mix, strain again, and bottle.

Peach Brandy.—Slice 1 ½ lb. of peaches; bruise half the stones of same, put them together in a jar; add 1 quart of pure spirits; digest for one month; add 1 lb. best refined sugar; in a few days strain with pressure; clear; add a few drops orange flower; bottle for use.

Imperial Peach Brandy.—Take 2 ½ oz. powdered bitter almonds, 1 ½ gallon of alcohol, 2 ½ gallons of water; mix; macerate for 24 hours; add strained syrup of 2 lbs. of sugar, 1 pint of peach jelly, 3 oz. preserved ginger, juice and peel of one lemon; digest; in two or three days strain clear.

Raspberry or Strawberry Liqueur.—Take 2 gills of the juice of either fruit, 2 gills of alcohol; macerate for six days; add ¼ pint of syrup, and, if agreeable, 1 drop essence of vanilla; strain.

Raspberry Brandy.—To a pint of water add in a covered vessel 1 quart of red or white raspberries, and 1 quart of brandy, 1 lb. of loaf-sugar; keep for one month; strain clear.

Hawthorn Ratafia.—Fill a bottle with the blossoms of the white thorn, free from husks; fill up with pale brandy; at the proper time add a few apricot kernels; strain in a fortnight; sweeten to taste.

Ratafia à la Violette.—Bruise 2 drachms of Florentine orris root; add 1 oz. of archel, 4 lbs. of sugar, and 2 pints of spirits of wine; in six weeks strain.

Orange Ratafia.—Into a jar put 9 mandarin or sweet oranges, a little cinnamon and coriander seed; add 2 quarts of brandy; in three months strain and bottle.

Rose Cordial.—Take 4 drops tinct. of musk, 2 drops oil of orange, 5 drops oil of roses; dissolve in 5 pints of gin; add ½ gallon clear syrup; colour with tincture of cochineal.

Rosolio.—To 12 drops essence of vanilla, 2 drops oil of roses, 5 drops essence of amber, dissolved in 1 quart of alcohol, add clear syrup of 2 lbs. of sugar in ½ gallon of water; colour with cochineal.

Sighs of Love.—Make a syrup of 3 lbs. of sugar to ½ gallon of water; add 1 pint of rose-water, 1 quart of rectified spirit, and 1 drop essence of ambergris.

Shrub.—Infuse in 1 gallon of rum or brandy the peels of 3 oranges and 3 lemons, and 1 quart of lemon juice; let this digest two months; then add some syrup and water; in four days strain clear. Or to 1 pint of rum add ½ gill each of lemon and orange juice, a small quantity of the peel, and sweeten to taste.

Sirop de Thé.—Make an infusion of 1 oz. of black tea and

3 oz. of green, with 1 pint of water; add 1 ½ lb. of sugar, and ¼ pint of pale brandy; strain while warm.

Ratafia d'Ecorces.—The thin peel of 2 Seville oranges; tincture of saffron, 1 drachm; neroli, 1 drop; proof spirit, 1 quart; sugar, 1 lb.; digest for two days.

Ratafia de Grenoble.—Take 6 lbs. of black-heart cherries and 2 lbs. of clean cherry leaves, half the peel of a citron or Seville orange; well bruise the cherries, breaking the stones; put the mixture in a jar; add the clean leaves, a lemon-peel, and 2 quarts of brandy; cover in 18 hours; strain; if not sufficiently flavoured, pour on for another twelve hours.

Ratafia de Café.—Fresh roasted coffee, ½ lb. ground; pounded loaf-sugar, ½ lb.; proof spirit, or brandy, 2 pints; digest for one week; filter and bottle.

Ratafia de Chocolat.—Fresh-roasted cocoa-nuts, 1 lb.; proof spirit, ½ gallon; digest for a fortnight; strain; add of loaf-sugar, 1 ½ lb.; tincture of vanilla, 30 drops.

Ratafia de Brou de Noix.—15 young walnuts, ripe for pickling, 1 pint brandy, ¼ lb. sugar; digest for four months; press out the liquor; filter; will be fit for use in six weeks.

Ratafia de Cassis.—Ripe black currants, 2 ½ lbs.; loaf-sugar, 1 ½ lb.; cloves and cinnamon, of each 1 drachm; proof spirit, 3 pints; digest three days; strain after cleaning.

Almond Syrup.—Beat 3 oz. of sweet and 2 oz. of bitter almonds, blanched in a marble mortar to a paste; add 2 tablespoonfuls of orange-flower water, ½ pint of cream, 1 pint of milk (thoroughly strain), with ½ pint of water; sweeten with clarified syrup to the taste; add ½ oz. gum arabic, dissolved in the milk, and ½ oz. spirits of wine.

Sirop d' Absinthe.—Macerate for 24 hours, or more, in 3 pints of water, ½ lb. of fresh wormwood tops (*Artemisia absinthium*); strain with pressure; add 4 pints of clarified syrup, and 1 tablespoonful of pure spirit.

Sirop d'Ananas.—½ pint of pine-apple juice, fermenting two days with the residue of the fruit; strain; add 1 lb. of sugar; boil for three minutes; skim, and strain clear.

Sirop de Capillaire.—Take 4 oz. Canadian maiden-hair fern (*Adiantum pedatum*), infused in 2 pints of boiling water; strain; add 5 pints clarified syrup; pour the boiling syrup over 2 oz. more of maiden-hair; re-infuse for two hours, and again strain.

Syrup of Cream, for Travelling.—Equal quantities of pounded loaf-sugar and cream, well mixed; bottled and closely corked and sealed in 2 oz. wide-mouth phials, so as to only open sufficient enough for a meal.

Syrup of Rose.—Use of damask-rose petals, 12 oz.; refined sugar, 3 lbs.; boiling water, 1 ½ pint; rectified spirit, 2 ½ fluid oz.; macerate the rose petals in the water for 12 hours; filter; evaporate in a water bath to 2 quarts; add the sugar; strain clear; when cold, add the spirit.

Syrup of Citric Acid.—1 oz. of citric acid dissolved in 1 oz. of water; tincture of lemon-peel, 30 drops; well mix; add 1 pint of syrup.

Syrup of Violets.—Macerate 1 ½ lb. fresh violet flowers, free from stalk, in 1 pint distilled soft water, for two days, closely covered; then press, strain, filter clear; add 2 lbs. of sugar; boil to a syrup; when cool, add ½ fluid oz. of spirit.

Syrup of Ginger.—To tincture of ginger, ½ fluid oz., add clarified syrup, ½ pint.

Syrup of Orange or Lemon Peel.—Tincture of orange-peel, 3 drachms; clarified syrup, ½ pint.

Syrup of Lemons.—Lemon-juice (strained), ½ pint; sugar, 2 ½ lbs.; rectified spirit, 2 fluid oz.; boil the juice ten minutes; strain; add the sugar; when cool, colour the spirit with saffron.

Imitation Lemon Syrup.—4 oz. tartaric acid; 2 drachms oil of lemon; 6 oz. powdered loaf-sugar.

Sirop de Gomme.—Make a solution with best gum arabic, with hot water; sweeten with syrup.

Usquebaugh, which is a strong compound liquor, chiefly taken as a dram, is made in the highest perfection at Drogheda, in Ireland. The following are the ingredients, and the proportions in which they are to be used: of best brandy, 1 gallon; raisins (stoned), 1 lb.; cinnamon, cloves, nutmeg, and cardamoms, of each, 1 oz., crushed in a mortar; saffron, ¼ oz.; rind of 1 Seville orange; brown sugar-candy, 1 lb.; shake all these well every day, for at least three weeks, then filter for use.

Vanilla Milk.—To 12 drops essence of vanilla, and 1 oz. of lump sugar, add 1 pint of new milk.

BITTER DRINKS

Irrespective of the use of bitter extracts specially resorted to for medical purposes, beverages are made in which the bitter principle of gentian, dandelion, hops, wormwood, quassia, orange-peel, calumba, cascarilla, and a few others, is greatly used. The custom of infusing bitter plants in vinous drinks is very ancient. Bitter drinks invariably present the bitter principle of some herb, such as wormwood, &c., which, when mixed with sundry other aromatics and spirits, and then distilled, makes the *Absinthe de Suisse* so popular in France and Switzerland; indeed, the Swiss seem particularly fond of bitters, for the very bitterest of bitters is one of their favourite liquors—viz., the spirit distilled from gentian root. The Americans have a few bitter liquors, of which Boker's and Angostura are decidedly the best. In England, the bitters of the public-houses are invariably made of spirit, from orange-peel, cassia, gentian, cardamom seeds, or any other bitter that fancy dictates. The well-known tonic or bitter-cup is made of quassia wood. It is reputed to be stomachic, and to assist digestion. The roasted chips of this wood form one of the ingredients used as a substitute for hops in embittering beer. No doubt, simple bitters are useful when occasionally taken in moderation, but their excessive use must be deplorably destructive to health.

Wine Bitters.—Take the thin peel of 1 lemon, 1 bitter orange; add 3 oz. Cape sherry, 2 oz. of water; infuse; this is a capital tonic.

American Stoughton Bitters.—16 oz. gentian root, 12 oz. orange-peel, 3 oz. Virginia snake-root, 1 oz. saffron, 1 oz. red saunders wood; grind these into a powder; add 1 gallon of rectified spirit; macerate for three weeks, constantly agitating for a fortnight; strain carefully; the last pint of liquor strain separately with pressure, and, when clear, add it to the clear spirit.

Spirituous Bitters.—To 3 oz. dried Seville orange-peel, add 2 oz. gentian root, and ½ oz. cardamom seeds; macerate in 1 ½ pint spirits of wine for a month.

Gentian Bitters, or Aromatic Wine.—Gentian, ½ oz.; yellow bark, 1 oz.; canella, 1 drachm; bitter orange-peel (dried), 2 drachms; proof spirit, ¼ pint; sherry, 1 pint; pound the ingredients together; add the spirit; digest for one month; add the wine in seven days; strain with pressure, and filter.

Brandy Bitters.—Orange-peel, 8 oz.; cardamoms, 1 oz.; cinnamon, 1 oz.; essence of cochineal, 2 drops; gentian root, 6 oz.; brandy, 1 gallon; digest for a month, strain with pressure, and filter.

Brandy Bitters, No. 2.—Digest in 1 quart of brandy, 3 oz. sliced gentian root, 3 oz. dried orange-peel, 1 oz. of cinnamon (bruised), 3 cloves, for one month; strain clear.

Bitters.—Raisins, 1 lb.; bruised cinnamon, 3 oz.; Virginia snake-root, 1 oz.; zest and juice of 1 orange and 1 lemon; cloves, 20; digest in rum for two months; strain.

Essence of Bitters.—¼ lb. orange-peel (dried), ¼ lb. orange-apples, ¼ lb. gentian root, ¼ lb. lemon-peel, ground to powder; macerate for ten days; add 1 gallon of pure spirit; strain with pressure; add 1 quart of soft water.

ALE AND BEER

"Inspiring bold John Barleycorn,
What dangers thou canst make us scorn!"

Beer is a liquor of great antiquity. The origin of the art of
brewing is ascribed by Herodotus to Isis, the excellent wife
of Osiris, King of Egypt. "It was Isis who chose the ox as her
type, on account of its usefulness in agriculture; from hence
the Egyptians fancied the soul after her death animated the
ox, and, impelled by this idea, they exalted that useful animal
to the rank of a deity." The statues of Isis represent her with
the body of a woman and head of an ox. Putting aside as
purely fabulous this notion of Herodotus, it is certain, at all
events, that beer was the favourite beverage of the ancient
Egyptians—the soil and climate not permitting the growth of
the grape for wine. The most celebrated beer of the period was
the potation made at Pelusium, a town near the mouth of the

Nile, about 1,200 years before the Christian era. The Romans, who learnt the art of brewing from the Egyptians, called this drink by the appropriate name of *cerevisia*, in honour of Ceres, the celebrated agricultural Queen of Sicily, who was afterwards deified as the Goddess of Plenty. That it was known to the Greeks, the writings of Xenophon and Aristotle furnish proof. It was at an early period the favourite potation of the Germans and Gauls, from whom it was introduced into England, and to this day it remains the most popular beverage with the bulk of the people. Beer is thus extolled by Warton:—

> "Balm of my cares, sweet solace of my toils,
> Hail! juice benignant! O'er the costly cups
> Of riot-stirring wine, unwholesome draught!
> Let Pride's loose sons prolong the wasteful night.
> My sober evening let the tankard bless,
> With toast embrown'd, and fragrant nutmeg fraught,
> While the rich draught, with oft-repeated whiffs
> Tobacco mild improves. Divine repast!
> Where no crude surfeit or intemperate joys
> Of lawless Bacchus reign; but o'er my soul
> A calm Lethean creeps; in drowsy trance
> Each thought subsides, and sweet oblivion wraps
> My peaceful brain, as if the magic rod
> Of leaden Morpheus o'er my eyes had shed
> Its opiate influence. What though sore ills
> Oppress, dire want of chill-dispelling coals,
> Or cheerful candle, save the makeweight's gleam
> Haply remaining; heart-rejoicing ale
> Cheers the sad scene, and every want supplies."

Ale was first made from malted barley alone. Beer (from the German word *bier*) was the name given long afterwards to ale flavoured with bitters, such as hops, &c. Hops were first introduced from Germany in the year 1524, during the reign of Henry VIII.:—

> "Turkies, carp, picarell, and beere,
> Came into England all in one year."

Ale-houses were first licensed in the reign of Charles II. That variety of beer called *Porter* derives its name from its consumption by the London porters, and other hard-working men. It was first called *Entire*, or entire butt, because drawn from one cask. The malt liquors previously in use were ale, beer, and twopenny. It was then customary to call for a tankard of three thirds (or three threads), which was a mixture of a third each of ale, beer, and twopenny. This obliged the drawer to go to three casks to supply a single tankard. To improve upon this system, a brewer named Harwood, in 1722, made a liquor he called *entire*, meaning a combination of the above three kinds. This was first retailed at the "Blue Last," Curtain Road, Shoreditch, and soon crept into popularity.

The origin of bottled beer is thus quaintly recorded by Fuller. "Dean Newall, of St. Paul's, in the reign of Queen Mary, was an excellent angler. But while Newall was catching of fishes, Bishop Bonner was bent on catching of Newall, and would certainly have sent him to the shambles had not a good London, merchant conveyed him away upon the seas. Newall was fishing on the banks of the Thames when he received the first intimation of his danger, which was so pressing that he dared not go back to his own house to make preparation for his flight. Like an honest angler, he had taken provisions for the day; and when, in the first years of England's deliverance, he returned to his own country, and his old haunts, he remembered that, on the day of his flight, he had left a bottle of beer in a safe place on the bank of the stream in which he had fished; there he looked for it, and 'found no bottle, but a gun,' for such was the sound emitted at the opening thereof." And this is supposed by many to be the origin of bottled ale in England. Dr. Pereira says, for medical purposes, that bottled porter is usually preferred to draught porter. It is useful as a restorative in the latter stages of fever, and to support the powers of the system after surgical operations, severe accidents, &c. Also that " beer considered dietetically possesses a three-fold property: it quenches thirst, it stimulates and cheers, and nourishes and strengthens; but if taken too copiously, is apt to intoxicate. The power of appeasing thirst depends upon the aqueous ingredient which it contains, assisted somewhat by its acid-ulous constituents (carbonic and acetic acid); its stimulating, cheering, or intoxicating power is derived, either wholly or principally, from the alcohol, which it contains from 2 to 8 per cent.; lastly, its nutritive or strengthening quality is derived from the sugar, dextrine, and similar substances contained in it; moreover, the bitter principle of hops confers on beer tonic properties. From these combined qualities, beer, if taken in moderation, proves a refreshing and salubri-ous drink, and is an agreeable and valuable stimulant, and a support to those who have to undergo much bodily fatigue."

Pure porter, says Dr. Ure, is a far more wholesome beverage for the people, when drunk in moderation, than the thin, acidulous wines of France and Germany.

The dark colour and strong taste of porter renders it easier of adulteration than ale.

That the popular beverage of bitter beer is not well adapted hygienically for general consumption has been insisted upon by medical writers. It is the opinion of Dr. A. S. Taylor and Dr. G. O. Rees, "that it may be greatly doubted whether any benefit can be derived from swallowing the strong bitter infusion (pale ale) now so largely consumed; and whether *positive mischief* may not be done by mixing an active therapeutical agent with the gastric juice, while the stomach is discharging its functions. The writers have had occasion to observe the evil which sometimes results from the practice, and sincerely hope that the present custom of ordering a powerful tonic with meals will soon fall into disuse."

Brewing, to be successfully practised, can only be learnt by experience; no treatise on the art can give that judgment that the practised brewer has, which enables him to contend with very many unexpected difficulties, arising from sudden changes of weather, fluctuations of temperature, and other causes which render modifications of treatment necessary, and which no precise rule can provide against. Yet a good treatise on the subject (Black's is excellent) will be found a valuable guide for affording a knowledge of the properties of the materials employed, and the principles of fermentation, and other essential particulars, which it would greatly exceed our limits to treat of. It is sufficient for our purpose thus briefly to describe the art of brewing:—The malt should first be crushed (in a malt mill), and macerated for a given time in hot water, the temperature of which ranges from 157° and upwards; during this process, called mashing, the peculiar azotized substance in the malt, known as diastase, acts upon the starch of the grain, and converts it into a mucilaginous substance and sugar. It is then strained, and the liquor, called "wort," boiled. As soon as the boiling begins hops (according to desired strength) are added. After undergoing this process the liquor is transferred into shallow coolers, and exposed to a good current of air, in order to prevent " souring." It is then *tunned*, and *yeast* added. This is the most critical point of brewing. When sufficiently *fermented*, it must be when necessary *cleansed*, and then stored. A slow fermentation succeeds, which strengthens the beer, and makes it less sweet; and causes it to become charged with carbonic acid gas.

The liquor, as the water used by brewers and others is termed, is of great importance; soft, or hard water softened by exposure, is generally preferred, because it makes a stronger extract, and is more inclined to ferment; but hard water makes the best keeping beer, and is less liable to turn sour. Sometimes the water requires to be softened by adding a spoonful of soda to a barrel; some use a handful of common salt mixed with an ounce of salt of tartar. We may add that the water which makes good tea makes good beer.

The famed ales of Burton-on-Trent are brewed with hard water, the river Trent containing an unusually large proportion of sulphate of lime, together with carbonate and muriate of lime. These salts exert a considerable depuritive power on vegetable juices, superseding the necessity for finings; thus the ale brewed by this water becomes bright and clear almost immediately. Burton ale is the strongest in general use.

The Scotch ales are distinguished for the small quantity of hops they contain, and for their vinous flavour. Those of Edinburgh, Prestonpans, and Belhaven are pre-eminent.

Strong ale is mostly made from the best pale malt, and the fermentation is allowed to take place slowly, so that the ferment is exhausted and separated. This, combined with the large amount of undecomposed sugar remaining, enables the liquor to keep long without requiring a large amount of hops.

India pale ale differs chiefly in being made with an extra supply of hops. Every county and town in England has its variety of ales, and beer; and even these varieties are subdivided, the difference consisting chiefly (the same quantity of malt and hops being employed) in the preparation of the malt.

Highly-coloured beer is made by adding to the malt a quantity, as may be desired, of strong dried and charred malt. The sugar which has been charred by the action of fire is termed "caramel," a French word. Porter and stout are so prepared.

Good, sound, honest English ale only can be produced by using a plentiful supply of good malt, combined with good liquor, hops and yeast, and clean utensils; with these and a little care and judgment, and good temper—for he who possesses no self-control ought not to brew—cannot fail to reward the operator with a splendid beverage: "Good ale needs no bush." October and March are the best brewing months, the temperature of the air then permitting the easy cooling of the wort. Old ale is best brewed in October.

To Fine Beer.—Take 1 oz. of isinglass, boiled in 2 quarts of beer; when dissolved and cooled put it in the beer, and stir with a stick. The beer so treated should be used soon, for the isinglass is apt to make the beer flat. A handful of hops boiled in 2 quarts of beer, and put in two days before the clarification, will greatly improve and assist the process. Or 3 drachms of calcined powdered alum may be used, dissolved in alcohol, and mixed with 10 gallons of the beer.

The quantity of malt requisite for a brewing depends upon the strength required. Malt ought to be crisp, tender, of sweet taste, full grain, and of thin skin. A simple test of good malt is this: take a tumbler nearly full of water, put in some malt; if it swims, it is good; if any sink to the bottom, that is not true malt. If malt is hard and feels like barley, it has not been well made, and will weigh heavier than that which has been properly made. Pale malt is the slowest and least dried, producing more wort than high-dried malt, and of better quality. Amber malt produces a flavour much admired in many malt liquors. Brown malt loses much of its nutritious qualities, but it confers a peculiar flavour on the beer. Roasted malt is used to give colour and flavour to porter. Ground malt is termed "grist" and when in the mash-tub it is called "goods" and the extract "wort." A bushel of good malt will measure 1 ¼ bushel when ground: a quarter yields 9 ½ to 10 bushels.

Hops contain a bitter resinous principle called "lupulin," which is its active principle. It has the property of preserving the beer, as well as of imparting to it a wholesome bitter taste. The best hops are packed in a solid mass, in bags called pockets, averaging 1 ½ cwt. each. New hops have a fine yellowish olive-green colour, and a rich fragrant sweet flavour. Of the many growths and qualities, those from Farnham, and Middle and East Kent, and Worcester, are the best. In the selection of hops much must depend on the use they are intended for. The finer class of ales demand a first-class hop; while the strong ales, porter, &c, are hopped with Sussex, Mid-Kent, &c. New hops are preferable to old ones; they lose their power by keeping.

In bottling beer, be careful to use clean dry bottles, and especially sound corks. The beer must be clear, and the bung of the cask should be drawn out the day before. After bottling, let the beer remain uncorked for a time, according to whether it is desired to keep it during hot or cold weather; use wire to secure the corks, and stow it in a cool place. October beer should not be bottled till March at the earliest, nor March beer till Christmas. Beer must not be bottled while showing a tendency to spurt from the bung-hole. Sometimes, when the beer is flat, a raisin or a little rice or sugar in the bottle will set the carbonic acid free.

In tapping beer, use a wooden mallet to drive the tap in, have the vent-peg loose while tapping, and remember to tilt the cask while running.

The beer cellar should not be too cold, or too exposed to draughts of hot air, but kept, as clean and airy as possible, regulating the temperature by air-shutters. As soon as the stock is laid in and fermentation ceases, knock in all the vent-pegs lightly, and keep the casks as secure from agitation as possible. A beer cellar under a roadway always suffers more or less from the vibration of passing vehicles, &c.

To Restore a Barrel of Stale, or Sour Beer.—Put ¼ lb. good hops, and 2 lbs. sound chalk in the bung-hole; stop it close, and in a few days it will draw off perfectly fresh; or a small teaspoonful of carbonate of soda may be mixed with every quart that is drunk. Many hang a linen bag in the cask, filled with burnt oyster-shells, pounded.

To Turn Porter into Stout.—Insert 4 gallons of molasses into a butt of porter, with 1 quart of finings, in a week draw off; tapping first in the middle of the butt.

To give Beer a Good Flavour.—Place 2 or 3 sea-biscuits in a bag, with some hops, and put these in the cask.

To give New Ale the Flavour of Old.—Take out the bung and put in a sliced Seville orange.

Malt liquors will ofttimes be protected from the effects of electricity by placing over the casks a rod of iron.

In cleansing brewing utensils, be careful not to use soap or any greasy material; a good brush and scalding water will generally thoroughly cleanse them, but all the fur on the sides or bottom must be removed; after this, they should be well drained, and left in some airy situation to sweeten. If they are still found to be tainted, take wood ashes, and boil them to a strong ley, which spread over the bottoms of the vessels scalding hot; then scrub with a brush or broom, or throw some stone lime into water in the vessel, and scrub over the bottom and sides, rinsing well with clean water. In some cases it is necessary to wash with oil of vitriol, diluted with seven or eight times its bulk of water. Fresh burnt charcoal can also be employed.

To Cure or Prevent Foxing.—Cut a handful of hyssop small, mix it with a handful of salt, and put it into a cask; then stir and stop close; or, infuse a handful of hops and a little salt of tartar in boiling water; when cold, strain the liquor off, and pour it into a cask, which bung up.

Yeast.—The best known is that of beer; it is a solid soft substance, of a greyish yellow colour, which dries to a pale brownish mass, and is nearly insoluble in water; it readily putrifies when moistened. This material has excited much attention amongst scientific people, but there can be no doubt but that it is created from the azotic portion of the grain during the process of fermentation; liquid free from azotized matter does not give yeast. The best yeast for working is that thrown out of the bung-holes of the casks; that from strong ale works slower, but is stronger than any other; it deteriorates by keeping, unless it is deprived, by means of straining with a good pressure, of all the liquid portion, leaving the residue a stiff clay-like paste; this, wrapped up in waxed paper or cloth, and put into tins, kept in a dry cool place, will retain its fermenting properties for some time, but it must not be suffered to become quite dry, for in that case it would become useless; by adding a little water to a portion of this paste (or German yeast), it will, if kept properly, be always ready for use. In places where yeast is not easily procurable, it is a common practice to twist sticks of wood, those of hazel in preference, so as to be full of openings, and to steep them in the yeast during fermentation. They are then dried, and used at the next brewing in the wort, instead of yeast.

Bad yeast may generally be restored by mixing it with a

little flour, salt, brandy, and beer. Good yeast can be made by adding the same mixture to the grounds of ale. An artificial yeast can also be made by adding 2 oz. of brown sugar to 1 lb. of well-mashed mealy potatoes, and 2 spoonfuls of common yeast, mixed with warm water, to a proper consistence, and kept warm while fermenting; this will yield a quart of good yeast.

Elbulum, or Elderberry Beer.—Boil in 18 gallons of the finest and strongest wort 1 ½ peck of elderberries, quite ripe; strain clear; when cold, work the liquor in the cask, and let it remain in the cask one year; bottle off: the addition of a few hops will be found an improvement, as will also a few spices, tied up in a muslin bag.

AERATED BEERS

Ginger Beer, No. 1.—To 1 ¼ oz. cream of tartar, add 1 ½ oz. Cochin ginger (bruised); 2 lbs. loaf-sugar; thin peel and juice of 2 lemons; bruise the ginger and lemon-peel with ½ lb. of sugar, in a mortar; put all together in a pan; add 6 quarts boiling water, and, when lukewarm, 2 table-spoonfuls of good ale yeast; let this ferment ten hours, drain clear, cork tight and tie down; will be fit for use in ten hours.

Ginger Beer, No. 2.—Bruise and macerate, in 1 gallon of water, 6 oz. of good African ginger and ½ oz. capsicum pods; boil the same slowly for two hours; when nearly cold, add 9 lbs. of loaf-sugar, 12 oz. cream of tartar, 1 oz. essence of lemons, mixed with 1 oz. spirits of wine; put all in a cask, and pour on 11 gallons of boiling water; when nearly cool, add the whites of 6 eggs, whisked with a little of the liquor, and sufficient yeast to ferment. If required, clear through tammy; strain; pass through filtering paper, which has a little magnesia over it; this is a long operation, but produces a fine article; have the tap driven in above the sediment; place the bottles on their sides in a cellar, as usual with ale, &c.

Ginger Beer, No. 3.—To 20 lbs. of sugar, add 20 thin lemon-peels, and strained juice of same; 16 oz. of bruised ginger; boil the sugar, ginger, and peel, in 6 gallons of water, half an hour; pour into a pan; add 12 gallons of water; strain into a barrel; add ½ oz. isinglass finings, and 1 bottle of pale brandy; when lukewarm, ferment with yeast.

Ginger Beer, Dr. Pereira's (for Hot Climates), No. 4.—Loaf-sugar, 5 lbs.; lemon-juice, ¼ pint; honey, ¼ lb.; bruised ginger, 5 oz.; water, 4 gallons; boil the ginger in 3 quarts of water for one hour; add the sugar, lemon-juice, and honey, with the remainder of the water; then strain clear; when cold, add the whisked white of an egg, and half a teaspoonful of essence of lemon; let it stand four days, then bottle for use.

Schultz's, No. 5.—10 gallons of boiling water, 10 oz. cream of tartar, 15 oz. ground ginger, 10 lemons cut in slices and boiled together; let them stand till nearly cool; strain and press them; dissolve in this mixture 15 lbs. of sugar, and add when lukewarm 1 pint of yeast; let the compound stand fourteen hours; skim and filter, bottle and bind the corks.

Schultz's, No. 6.—Take 22 lbs. of best refined white sugar; 1 quart of lemon or lime juice, 2 lbs. new honey, 2 lbs. bruised Jamaica ginger, 1 drop of citronelle, 2 drops of neroli, 18 gallons of filtered soft water, ½ oz. of fresh

expressed essence of lemon-peel; white of 1 egg, well
whisked; boil the ginger in sufficient water for one hour,
strain this clear, boil the residue in more water, till nearly
all the virtue is extracted; strain clear as possible, and add
to the first infusion; put in the water, juice, sugar, and
honey; well mix and filter clear through tammy; add the
essence, digested in a gill of spirit; pour in a clean cask,
with white of egg, agitate for one hour, and after four days
bottle. If desired to be fermented, add ½ pint good yeast,
and let it work while lukewarm.

Ginger Beer, or Imperial Pop, No. 7.—Take cream of tartar,
3 ½ oz.; powdered ginger, 4 oz.; sugar, 2 lbs.; lemon-juice,
2 ½ oz.; water, 2 gallons; digest when lukewarm; add 1 oz.
of German yeast; skim, and bottle tight.

Ginger Beer Extemporaneous, No. 8.—Concentrated essence
of ginger, 2 drops; clean syrup, ½ oz.; teaspoonful lemon-
juice, all mixed together in a glass; rub the edge of the
glass with lemon-peel, and fill up with water from the
seltzogene, or a bottle of soda-water, or mix the above
formula in a bottle, adding aërated water from machine.

Ginger Beer, with Raisins, No. 9.—To 1 lb. of raisins, add ½ lb.
of sugar, 1 oz. bruised ginger, ¾ oz. citric acid in powder;
macerate the raisins and ginger in 2 quarts of water for
one day, then boil for one hour; add the sugar; strain with
pressure, adding the citric acid; bottle tight.

Ginger Beer, for keeping longer than Twelve Months, No. 10.—
Jamaica ginger (bruised), 3 ½ oz.; loaf-sugar, 4 lbs.; thin
peel and juice of 2 lemons; citric acid (in powder), 2 oz.;
German yeast, 2 oz.; boiling water, 2 gallons; essence of
capsicum, 10 drops; macerate the ginger in 1 quart of the

water for one day; add the sugar and 2 quarts of water; boil together; strain while warm; boil the residue in 1 quart of water; strain; add to the liquor and rest of the water, which pour boiling hot on the lemon and acid; when lukewarm, add the capsicum and yeast on a crust of bread; let it ferment two or three days, according to temperature; strain clear; add ¼ pint of alcohol; and bottle in a fortnight.

To aërate Ginger Beer and other Drinks.—Dissolve in 1 gallon of water 2 drachms essence of ginger, and ¼ pint of lemon-juice, 2 drops essence of lemon-peel; when well mixed, bottle in ginger beer bottles, filling only to the shoulder; add to each bottle ½ drachm of bicarbonate of soda; drive in cork, and string immediately.

Spruce Beer.—Sugar, 1 lb.; essence of spruce, 1 oz.; boiling water, 1 gallon; add, when lukewarm, a tablespoonful of German yeast; ferment, and bottle like ginger beer.

White Spruce Beer.—To 1 ½ pint of essence of white spruce add 3 gallons of boiling water and 6 lbs. of loaf-sugar; ferment with yeast, and use same formula as in ginger beer.

Spruce Beer.—To 6 gallons of water, add 2 quarts of molasses, 3 oz. of hops, 2 oz. allspice, ¾ lb. bruised ginger, 6 oz. of essence of spruce; boil the ginger, hops, and allspice in the water for one hour; stir in the molasses and spruce; strain while warm into a cask; stir in ½ pint good yeast; when the fermentation ceases, bung up the cask; in six days draw from tap and bottle.

Sarsaparilla or Lisbon Diet Beer.—Infuse 1 ½ oz. compound extract of sarsaparilla in 1 ½ pint of water; when cold, add 8 pints of good Burton beer.

Treacle Beer.—In 8 quarts of boiling water put 1 ½ lb. of

treacle, ¼ oz. bruised ginger, 3 bay leaves, and 1 oz. of hops; boil the infusion an hour; ferment with 1 oz. yeast, placed on a slice of bread; when fermenting is finished, either bottle or keep it in a cask.

CIDER AND MEAD

Cider (*Pomaceum*) is the fermented juice of the apple; it is, like beer, a liquor of great antiquity, being mentioned by Pliny. Of the produce of the different cider-making districts, the cider of Normandy ranks highest; Herefordshire, Devon, Somerset, and New Jersey in the United States, are also celebrated for good cider.

To make Good Cider.—Take as much fruit (24 bushels to the hogshead of 63 gallons) as will make sufficient juice to fill a cask; mash into a pulp, spread the pulp so as to cover a large surface in the open air for 24 hours; press out the juice as clear as possible; fill the barrel up to the bung-hole, and keep it filled up as the fermentation proceeds, by adding fresh juice kept for the purpose; when the fermentation is ended, draw off into a clean barrel, which has had some brimstone burnt in it, by hanging an iron vessel through the bung-hole, and burning 1 drachm of brimstone in it; bung up tight, and keep the barrel of cider in a cool place.

Scotch Method of making Cider.—The apples are reduced to mucilage by beating them in a stone trough, similar to those used for watering horses, with pieces of ash-poles used in the manner that potatoes are mashed. The press consists of a strong box 3 feet square, and 20 inches deep, perforated on each side with auger holes. It is placed on a frame of wood, projecting 3 inches beyond the base of the box; a groove is cut in this projector 1 ½ inch wide and 1 inch deep, to convey the juice when pressed out of the box into the receiving pail. This operation is performed in the following manner: the box is filled alternately with strata of fresh straw and mashed fruit in the proportion of 1 inch of straw to 2 inches of mucilage; these are piled up a foot higher than the top of the box, and care is taken in packing the box itself to keep the fruit and straw about 1 inch from the sides of the box, which allows the juice to escape freely, and a considerable quantity of the liquor will run off without any pressure. This must be applied gradually at first, and increased regularly towards the conclusion. A box of the above dimensions will require about 2 tons weight to render the residuum completely free of juice.

The necessary pressure is obtained very easily, and in a powerful manner, by the compound levers pressing upon a lid or sink made of wood, about two inches thick, and rendered sufficiently strong by two cross-bars. It is made to fit the opening of the box exactly; and, as the levers force the lid down, they are occasionally slacked or taken off, and blocks of wood are placed on the top of the lid, to permit the levers to act, even after the lid has entered the box itself. Additional blocks are repeated, until the whole juice is extracted. The pressure may be increased more or less, by adding or diminishing the weight suspended at the extremity of the lever.

The liquor thus obtained is allowed to stand undisturbed twelve hours, in open vessels, to deposit sediment. The pure juice is then put into clean casks, and placed in a proper situation to ferment, the temperature being from forty-five to sixty degrees. The fermentation will commence sooner or later, depending chiefly on the temperature of the apartment where the liquor is kept; in most cases, during the first three or four days, but sometimes it will require more than a week to begin this process. If the fermentation begins early and proceeds rapidly, the liquor must be racked off, and put into fresh casks in two or three days; but if this does not take place at an early period, and proceeds slowly, five or six days may elapse before it is racked. In general, it is necessary to rack the liquor at least twice. If, notwithstanding the fermentation continues briskly, the racking must be repeated, otherwise the vinous fermentation, by proceeding too far, may terminate in acetous fermentation, when vinegar would be the result.

In racking off the liquor, it is necessary to keep it free of sediment and the *scum* or yeast produced by the fermentation. A supply of spare liquor must be reserved to fill up the barrels occasionally, while the fermentation continues. As soon as this ceases the barrels should be bunged up closely, and the bungs covered with rosin, to prevent the admission of air. If the cider is weak, it should remain in the cask about nine months; if strong, twelve or eighteen months is necessary before it should be bottled (*Farmers' Mag.* Vol. IX).

Perry is made similarly to cider from pears, which must be dry. The best pears for this purpose are seldom fit for eating, and the redder they are the better.

Mock Cider.—Take 14 lbs. of raisins with the stalks, wash them clean, by pouring on water; when ready, put them into a clean cask, with the head out, and pour in 6 gallons of soft clean water on them; bung up for fourteen days, then rack off in a clean cask, which is tapped; in six days it will be fit for bottling; when in bottle a week, it will be fit for use; use a little cochineal to colour, ere bottling; the raisins can be used afterwards for vinegar.

Sparkling Champagne Cider.—Put 10 gallons of good clear old cider into a strong clean beer barrel, pitched inside; add 3 pints clean syrup, and 5 oz. of tartaric acid. In ten minutes take the bung in one hand, and quickly add 7 ½ oz. of bicarbonate of potassa; bung up as tight as possible immediately.

Champagne Cider.—Put in a cask 18 gallons of cider, 3 pints of rectified spirit, and 5 pints of syrup; in three weeks' time fine with 1 pint of skimmed milk, 1 gill of orange-flower water—3 drops of neroli will improve it; bottle in Champagne bottles, and tie down with wire.

To Improve Rough Cider.—Take new cider from the press; mix it with as much honey or sugar as will support an egg; boil gently for fifteen minutes; skim it well, and when cool tun it, but do not quite fill; it will be fit for use in six weeks, and it will not get sweeter by keeping longer.

Metheglin is a very ancient and popular drink in the

north of Europe. The term is derived from the Welsh (Meddyglin). It is often confounded with mead, which is made from honeycombs.

"Our drowsy metheglin
Was ordained only to inveigle in
The nonce that knows not to drink yet,
But is fuddled before he can think it."

To make Metheglin.—To some new honey (that which runs from the comb is best) add spring water; put in an egg; boil this liquor till the egg swims above the liquor; strain, clear, pour in cask; to every 15 gallons add 2 oz. of bruised ginger, 1 oz. cloves and mace, 1 ½ oz. cinnamon, all bruised together and tied up in a muslin bag; accelerate the fermentation with yeast; when worked sufficiently, bung up; in six weeks draw off into bottle.

To make Mead.—Boil the combs from which the honey has been drained with sufficient water to make a tolerably sweet liquor; ferment this with yeast; proceed as per previous formula.

Sack Mead is made by adding a handful of hops and sufficient brandy to the comb liquor.

AERATED WATERS AND LEMON SHERBETS

Soda-Water and other Aerated Draughts owe their effervescence to carbonic acid gas; they are in much request
during hot weather to allay thirst, and in a feverish con-
dition of the human frame. Many natural mineral waters
are aërated. Mineral waters are divided into four classes:
carbonated (as Seltzer, &c.); chalybeate (as Cheltenham,
&c.); Saline (as Seidlitz, &c.); sulphurous (as Harrogate,
&c.).

Aerated Chalybeate Water (*Aqua chalybeata*) contains proto-
sulphate of iron, and bicarbonate of potassa; it is an easy
and excellent mode of introducing iron into the blood,
and is much recommended on that account, possessing
equal tonic properties to that of the natural springs.

Carrara, or Carbonated Lime Water, is an aërated solution of bicarbonate of lime; the best is made from calcined Carrara marble, each bottle containing 8 to 10 grains of carbonate of lime; it is administered to strengthen the bony structure.

Lithia Water is a solution of the freshly precipitated carbonate of lithia (*Lithia carbonas*); this water is becoming popular, being very useful in calculous complaints.

Magnesian Water is useful in indigestion, &c; being an aërated solution of carbonate of magnesia, it is an agreeable mode of taking magnesia.

Potass Water is a solution of bicarbonate of potass in distilled water, and aërated with washed carbonic acid gas.

Soda-Water is properly a solution of crystallized carbonate of soda, in distilled water, aërated with washed carbonic acid gas, upon the purity of which the excellence of this article mainly depends. That made by Messrs, Rawlings, and other eminent makers, contains from 4 to 15 grains of crystallized carbonate of soda in each bottle (all proportions in excess of 4 grains being usually prepared from a medical prescription). When employed as an anti-acid, it is highly important to obtain this article good.

Seltzer Water is carbonate of soda, common salt (chloride of sodium), and carbonate of magnesia.

In order to make aërated waters properly, it is absolutely necessary to possess a powerful aërating and bottling machine, and the water must be, with the carbonic acid gas and chemicals, of the purest quality; the corks used must also be excellent and prepared.

The Seltzogene is a very useful machine for aërating water or beverages of any description; it differs from, and is an improvement upon, the Gazogene: being made without joint of one piece of glass, which renders the apparatus free from leakage. They are, with ordinary care, managed with ease, and directions are always fully given from the maker, or from whom purchased. When bottled soda-water is not attainable, either for use on board ship, or for the colonies, these machines are very valuable.

Charges for the Quart Seltzogene.—13 scruples of tartaric acid (in white paper), in crystals; 16 scruples of bicarbonate of soda, in powder (in blue paper). For the three-pint, use 18 scruples of tartaric acid (in crystal) and 22 scruples of bicarbonate of soda. For the five-pint, use 26 scruples of bicarbonate of soda. Care must be taken to let off by the tap all the carbonic acid gas, before re-charging the apparatus. To imitate seltzer water, add, for the quart size, 4 scruples of Rochelle salts to the water in the lower globe. For the three-pint, use 6 scruples (2 scruples for each pint). Potash water—20 grains of carbonate of potash to each pint of water. Soda or Vichy—20 grains of bicarbonate of soda to each quart. Ginger Beer and Lemonade can be made with diluted syrup of ginger, or lemon, in a soda-water tumbler, and filled up with aërated water.

*

Various German mineral waters, especially Seltzer, Schwalbacher Weinbrunnen, Fachingen are in great request—Seltzer pre-eminently: this is sometimes drunk either as a beverage by itself, or mixed with wine or brandy. It is sparkling and clear, and of a pleasant, slightly acidulated taste; and it is prescribed, moreover, by the Faculty for many disorders, such as indigestion, &c. It contains chloride of sodium, bicarbonate of lime, soda and magnesia, carbonic acid, and a small quantity of iron. Schwalbacher Weinbrunnen is a ferruginous water, useful in cases of debility, and for the improvement of impoverished blood; it contains bicarbonate of iron, magnesia, soda, lime, &c. Fachingen is an acidulated, gaseous, and alkaline water, used in gouty and nervous habits, dyspepsia, heartburn, &c, and is a pleasant and refreshing beverage.

Effervescent Draught.—Carbonate of potash, 80 grains; pulverized citric acid, 17 grains; keep separate; when required for use, add 1 drop essence of lemon; dissolve in separate tumblers; mix; drink while effervescing.

Effervescent Draught, No. 2.—Bicarbonate of potash in solution 1 scruple; fresh lemon-juice (cleared), 4 drachms; water, 1 oz.

Effervescent Draught, No. 3.—Carbonate of soda, 30 grains; tartaric acid, 25 grains; tincture of calumba, 15 drops; syrup of orange-peel, 2 fluid drachms; water distilled, 2 fluid oz. Mix these ingredients, except the tartaric acid, in the water; mix the tartaric acid in another tumbler, with two table-spoonfuls of water; pour in the previous mixture, and drink while effervescing.

Citratic Kali.—Carbonate of soda, 2 oz.; tartaric acid (or citric), 2 ½ oz.; powdered loaf-sugar, 6 oz.; essence of lemon, 1 scruple; oil of orange, 1 scruple; neroli, 1 scruple; pound the sugar; add the oils and essence; mix the soda and acid well; when dry, bottle; cork tight; add dessert-spoonful in a soda-water-glassful of water.

Sherbet.—Powdered white sugar, 1 lb.; carbonate of soda, 2 oz.; tartaric acid, 3 oz.; essence of lemon, 1 drachm; mix well a teaspoonful of the powder in a tumbler of cold water. Very refreshing.

Imperial.—Lemon-peel, ½ oz.; cream of tartar, ½ oz.; loaf-sugar, 4 oz.; bruise the lemon-peel with the sugar; mix with the cream of tartar; bottle ; when required for use, add 1 pint boiling water.

Effervescent Acidulated Syrup of Lemon.—Loaf-sugar, 1 lb.; citric acid, 1 ½ oz.; essence of lemon, 16 drops. Pound the sugar and acid together; add the essence; make a syrup with ½ pint of water; add a little carbonate of soda in the tumbler, when required to be drunk.

A Seidlitz Powder.—Rochelle salts, 3 drachms; carbonate of soda, 25 grains; tartaric acid, 20 grains; mix the salt and soda in a blue paper, with the acid in a white paper. This is sufficient for ½ pint of water.

Seidlitz Powders.—Rochelle salt, 3 oz.; carbonate of soda, 1 oz.; mix and put 2 drachms and 2 scruples each in a blue paper; tartaric acid, ½ drachm, in each corresponding white paper.

Soda-Water Powders.—Bicarbonate of soda, 30 grains, in a blue paper; citric acid, 24 grains, in a white paper; mix each separately in nearly half a tumbler of water; pour the acid solution on the soda; drink immediately.

Chalybeated.—By adding 1 grain dried proto-sulphate of iron to the acid, it makes an agreeable refreshing tonic.

Refrigerent Draught.—Carbonate of potash, 1 scruple; syrup of orange-peel, 1 drachm; spirit of nutmeg, ½ drachm; distilled water, 12 drachms; tablespoonful of lemon-juice; mix; drink while effervescing.

Lemon Sherbet, No. 1.—White sugar, 3 lbs.; carbonate of soda, 1 lb.; essence of lemon, 2 ½ drachms; mix; put 3 drachms in each blue paper; make as many corresponding powders of ½ drachm of tartaric acid each.

Lemon Sherbet, No. 2.—Rub the zest of a lemon with a lump of sugar; the sugar must not exceed ½ oz. (or one drop of essence of lemon on same); pound it with 12 grains of citric acid; mix with a glass of water.

Lemon Sherbet, No. 3.—White sugar, powdered, 5 lbs.; citric acid, 2 oz.; essence of lemon-grass, 1 drachm; essence of neroli, 1 drachm; essence of lemon, 3 drachms; mix it into 2 ½ drachm papers, and preserve in a dark-coloured bottle, well corked, each powder sufficient for a glass of lemonade; it can be aërated by the addition of some bicarbonate of soda.

Lemon Sherbet, No. 4.—10 oz. powdered tartaric acid, 4 lbs. 6 oz. powdered sugar, 1 drachm oil of lemon; mix well together; keep dry. Half ounce of the first of these in one tumbler of water; dissolve ½ oz. of the next, put into a tumbler, and mix together.

Lemon Sherbet, No. 5.—Powdered sugar, sifted, 4 lbs.; citric acid, 1 oz.; essence of lemon, 2 drachms; thoroughly mix. Two teaspoonfuls of the powder make a very agreeable extemporaneous lemonade.

Orange Sherbet.—Well mix together 1 lb. of pounded sugar, 2 drops of neroli, 5 drops essence of orange-peel; ½ oz. citric acid; aërate, if required, with carbonate of soda.

Aerated Lemonade.—To each bottle put 1 fluid oz. of good lemon syrup; fill at the bottling-machine with aërated water; some use a mixture of diluted citric acid, essence of lemon, and sugar, but the syrup is most refreshing and palatable.

Magnesian Lemonade.—Crystallized citric acid, 18 grains; carbonate of magnesia, 12 grains; mix in tumbler of cold water. A pleasant saline.

Magnesian Lemonade.—Sulphate of magnesia, 1 oz.; bicarbonate of soda, 1 oz.; tartaric acid, ½ oz.; powdered loaf-sugar, ½ oz.; mix; put into a dry bottle for use.

Milk Lemonade, No. 1.—Take 6 lemons and 1 Seville orange; slice them, and powder over them 1 lb. of loaf-sugar; pour on a pint of boiling water and a pint of white wine; let stand for six hours covered; strain; pour in pint of boiling milk; strain till clear.

Milk Lemonade, No. 2.—Sugar, ½ lb.; water, 1 pint; dissolve together juice of 3 lemons; milk, 1 pint; strain through a hair sieve.

Milk Lemonade, No. 3.—To 1 lb. of loaf-sugar add 1 pint of water, 1 gill of lemon-juice, ½ pint of sherry; add 1 quart new milk; stir and strain.

Orgeat Lemonade, an American Drink.—Half wine-glass orgeat syrup, juice of half a lemon (strained); fill the tumbler one-third full of shaven ice; add ingredients;

balance to top with ice; rub the rim of glass with lemon-peel.

Ginger Lemonade.—Boil 12 ½ lbs. of sugar in 10 gallons of water for 20 minutes; clear with whites of eggs; bruise 10 oz. of ginger; boil with the liquor; add the juice of 10 lemons, and the thin peel of same; when cold, put into a cask with 2 tablespoonfuls of yeast and ½ oz. of isinglass. Next day, bung up; ready in a fortnight.

Lemonade.—Pare 6 lemons, 2 Seville and 1 Tangerine oranges very thin; pound them into a mass in a mortar with 2 lbs. of sugar; add 2 quarts of boiling water, the juice of 18 lemons, and 8 sweet and 2 Seville oranges; stir the whole well; strain clear; add orange-flower water to taste; a little lemon brandy is an improvement.

Lemonade.—Juice of 3 lemons, strained, peel of 1; sugar, ¼ lb.; cold water, 1 quart; mix; digest for five hours; strain through a sieve.

Lemon Syrup.—Citric acid, 1 ½ drachm; essence of lemon, 10 drops; sugar, 4 oz.; cold water, 1 pint.

Lemon Syrup, No. 2.—Citric acid, 2 ½ oz.; distilled water, 2 ½ oz.; tincture of lemon-peel, 5 ½ drachms; syrup, 3 pints; dissolve the acid and sugar in the water; add the tincture.

Lemon Whey.—Pint of boiling milk, ½ pint of lemon-juice; sugar to taste; mix; strain through sieve.

Lemon Shrub.—Juice of 12 lemons, thin rind of 2; 1 lb. of loaf-sugar, whites of 2 eggs well whisked, pint of water, ½ pint of rum, ½ pint of brandy; strain when required.

Lemon Syllabubs.—To 1 pint of cream, add pint of white wine, thin peel of 3 lemons, juice of 1 lemon, 1 lb.

powdered sugar; whip up well with 1 white of egg, and collect the froth off on a sieve. When served, put the liquor in glasses, and some froth on top.

King's Cup.—Peel of 1 lemon; lump sugar, 1 ½ oz.; cold water, 1 pint; teaspoonful of orange-flower water. After 10 hours' infusion, strain.

REFRIGERATION

Refrigeration, the name applied to the operation of cooling. The use of ice in this and other countries is becoming one of the necessaries of life; its uses in the preservation of articles of food, cooling of liquors, &c, and for medical and other purposes, are too well known to demand much introduction. An excellent mode of preserving ice for domestic use is by the refrigerator (or portable ice-chest); the possession of a good refrigerator, as regards the amount of comfort and luxury it brings, cannot be over-estimated; for icing wines and beverages it has a special advantage, the temperature can be adjusted at pleasure, while the contents are not wasted or spoiled.

To Ice Wines, &c.—In iceing wines or cups, it is merely necessary to place the vessel in the refrigerator, and the temperature required can be regulated by the length of time it remains, or by placing it in direct contact with the ice, or otherwise.

To Remove the Iced Beverage from the Refrigerator.— Remember, however, on removing the wine, &c, from the refrigerator, to wrap it round with a wet cloth. That the usual mode of exposing liquid which has been cooled immediately to the effect of warm air, without such protection, is decidedly unphilosophical and bad in practice, is shown thus:—

Immerse a thermometer in cold water, and on taking it out it will be found to sink several degrees; but it will immediately rise to the temperature of the air. Wrap a wet cloth, however, round the bulb of the thermometer, and it will retain its cool state till the cloth dries.

It is necessary to use care in selecting an ice-chest or refrigerator, for those badly made only assist in melting, instead of preserving, the ice. Those of the Wenham Lake Ice Company* (who first introduced them into this country in 1845) are both trustworthy and of excellent workmanship. This company has recently introduced an excellent vessel called "The American Double Wall Ice-Water Pitcher" which is suitable for claret and all kinds of cups and cool beverages. They are in general use in America, and only require to be known here to be in as great request as in that country. They afford always a draught of deliciously cool water, by being filled from the spring and kept at hand. By means of the double wall and the self-acting valve, the contents of the pitcher are completely shut off from the influence of the surrounding atmosphere; and so complete is the isolation, that by experiment 1 ½ lb. of Wenham Lake

---

* 140, Strand, London, W.C.

ice, put into 3 pints of water in the pitcher, at 71° Fahrenheit, took seven hours to melt, the water remaining cold for many hours afterwards. The same principle renders them as useful for hot water in winter as for iced water in summer, as they can be used as a substitute for the urn in summer at the tea-table, if not otherwise required. The Water Carafe Freezer, or Improved Champagne Frappé Pail, is a great acquisition in a family.

The Patent Freezing Jug consists of two cylinders, the outer being a double case forming the jug, in which is put a small quantity of cold spring water; the inner cylinder is then inserted, causing the water to rise to the top of the jug, completely surrounding the tube. Into this tube, by means of a funnel, is put a certain quantity of freezing powder, and cold water added, till the tube is full. By stirring and agitating the freezing liquid in the tube for fifteen minutes, the water in the jug will be frozen. Then pour out the freezing mixture (it is useless after one application), fill the tube with warm water, and the iced mass will come out; break up and bottle. This jug is sold at 315, Oxford Street, London.

To Ice Water.—Fill water caraffes, or clean wine bottles, with clean spring water, nearly up to the shoulder. (If they are filled full they are liable to burst.) Stop up the mouths, and let them stand at a fair distance apart, so that the ice mixture will have effect individually; in a pan or tub pound as much rough ice as required to fill up the tub, and to every 12 lbs. of ice add 3 lbs. of salt; put in this mixture, taking care it does not reach above one-third the height of the bottle, or else they will possibly break from too much frigid force; throw a wet cloth over the vessel; in about two hours the water will be well frozen; if in too compact a mass, let the bottles stand in cold water, with the mouths open.

We have already adverted to the valuable qualities possessed by the refrigerators of the Wenham Lake Ice Company, but it is only fair to the patentees of the "Dry Cold Air Refrigerators" to point out the peculiar advantages which they claim as belonging to their invention. The refrigerators made by Messrs. Chavasse and Co., 505, Oxford Street, it is asserted, not only pre serve the ice longer than any others, but they have the great advantage of maintaining a perfectly dry atmosphere: a most important feature, without which provisions cannot be preserved in their natural state.

To make Snow Ice.—Break some lake ice into small pieces, wrap them in a coarse strong cloth, and pound the mass into snow.

Ice Planes are useful in preparing shaving ice for juleps, cobblers, and other drinks.

To Break Ice use a sharp-pointed instrument, similar to a brad-awl, but with longer blade; the sharper the point, the easier the ice is broken.

In Freezing, a thermometer is of great service—the freezing point is below 32°. A good strong tub is best for use for ice and salt. Salt is used not to preserve ice, but to generate a greater degree of cold. A mixture of 12 lbs. of broken ice to 3 lbs. of salt is that most generally used. Use no other but the purest lake ice in drinks, or you will probably spoil them. Where ice is not obtainable, an efficient freezing powder is a valuable substitute. Freezing powders must be kept as dry as possible, or else they deteriorate. The mixture should be made in as thick a vessel as possible, to check external heat. When it is necessary to augment the power of freezing the mixture, you can double the charge, diluted with sufficient quantity of fresh water; but fresh powders put dry into the exhausted liquor will have no effect.

Freezing Mixtures can be thus made:—

No. 1.—Muriate of ammonia, 1 lb.; saltpetre (crushed), 1 lb. ; common soda, 2 lbs.; well pound together (dry); put the bottles into a vessel, add the mixture; agitate well, and cover with wet cloth; in half an hour the drink or wine is ready.

No. 2.—2 lbs. snow, or pounded ice; 3 lbs. crystallized chloride of calcium. This salt of lime produces intense cold.

No. 3.—4 lbs. sulphate of soda (Glauber's salts); 2 ½ lbs. hydrochloric acid (muriatic acid).

No. 4.—1 lb. nitrate of ammonia (this salt can be used again, if evaporated till dry); 1 lb. carbonate of soda ; 1 pint of water.

No. 5.—10 oz. sal-ammonia; 10 oz. saltpetre; 16 oz. Glauber's salts; 2 pints of water.

TEMPERATE BEVERAGES

TEA

Tea is the decoction made from the dried leaves of the varieties of the plant *Thea*, which is a native of Japan and China, known as *Thea*, *Bohea*, and *Thea Viridis*, and another species, *Thea Assamica*, commonly called Assam tea, grown in Assam in the Presidency of Bengal. In growth and form of leaf the plant resembles the myrtle. Its blossoms are white, similar to our wild rose, and very fragrant. The seeds of the berries yield an aromatic oil. Tea contains *theine*, an alkaloid similar to *caffeine* and *theobroma*. The best known varieties are, of black teas, Bohea, Congou, Souchong, and Pekoe. Orange pekoe owes its delicious perfume and flavour to being scented with the blossoms of an olive (*Olea fragrans*); and the flowers of the *Tasminum sambic* and *Gardenia florida* are also used to scent Souchong teas. Green teas, as Twankay,

Hyson, and Gunpowder (the finest consists of the unopened leaf-bud of the green variety of the *Thea*). Cowslip Hyson is flavoured by mixing with it the berries of *Chloranthus*, or by alternate layers of tea and dried cowslip flowers, and then sifted. Black tea has more sedative, green more stimulating, properties. "The use of tea and coffee (says Liebig) is not a matter of mere habit, but it is in some degree essential, it being a question if we had neither tea nor coffee, whether the popular instinct would not soon crave for, and find some substitute." Raynal observes, "The use of tea has contributed more to the sobriety of the Chinese than the severest laws, the most eloquent discourses, or the best treatise on morality." Its social properties no one understood better than Cowper, who thus eulogizes a comfortable evening at home:—

> "Now stir the fire, and close the shutters fast,
> Let fall the curtains, wheel the sofa round,
> And while the bubbling and loud-hissing urn
> Throws up a steamy column, and the cups
> That cheer but not inebriate wait on each;
> So let us welcome peaceful evening in."

A Chinese legend relates, that a pious hermit, who, in his watchings and prayers, had often been overtaken by sleep, so that his eyelids closed, in holy wrath against the weakness of the flesh cut them off, and threw them on the ground. But a god caused a tea shrub to spring out of them; the leaves, which exhibit the form of an eyelid, bordered with lashes, possess the gift of hindering sleep. Chinese writers tell us, that tea is of a cooling nature; if indulged too freely, it will produce exhaustion and lassitude; if too strong, it acts on the nerves injuriously. The Chinese themselves rarely consume any other than black tea. The Russians seldom use any but green. They are partial to a squeeze of a lemon in their tea, instead of milk or sugar.

By some, the use of tea is condemned in unqualified terms; by others, it has ascribed to it extraordinary virtues. The middle view will perhaps be the most just. "Tea in general does more harm, from the quantity of unnecessary liquid which it introduces into the stomach," says Dr. Mayo, "than by its specific qualities. Unnecessary liquid weakens the stomach, and turns to wind." Green tea is more apt to affect the nerves of the stomach than black tea, especially when drunk without milk, or without eating something. Tea, drunk at a late hour, or in large quantities, is apt to provoke watchfulness; but, if used in moderation, it is productive of soothing and happy effects on the mind and system—exhilarating, without intoxicating and exciting the brain to activity.

Weak tea is very relaxing, and therefore a little, and that good, is far better than the hot-water-bewitched and tea-begrudged infusion sometimes drunk. One teaspoonful for each person and "one for the pot" is a generally approved and adopted plan for one brewing, which, if drunk at the correct moment, gives you all the flavour of the tea and less of the bitter principle. The use of carbonate of soda to draw the tea is objectionable, and should be avoided; should the water, however, be hard, it will materially assist the infusion. The boiling point of water is 212°. Liquids do not get any hotter after they begin to boil, however long the boiling is continued.

COFFEE

> "Coffee, which makes the politician wise,
> And see all things with his half-shut eyes.
>
> —POPE."

Coffee.—This well-known beverage is an infusion of the burnt berries of the coffee-tree (*Coffea Arabica*), an evergreen shrub, which is indigenous to Arabia and countries bordering on the Red Sea, "where it is much cultivated. It is also now grown in many parts of the world which admit of its successful cultivation. Bruce tells us it is a native of Abyssinia, and that he found it growing wild in great abundance from Cassa to the banks of the Nile. The story told of its introduction is, that the prior of an Arabian monastery, being informed by his goatherd of the effect produced on the goats when they happened to browse on the coffee-tree, gave an infusion of the berries to his monks, to prevent their inclination to sleep, which frequently interfered with the due performance of the nocturnal prayers. Another account is, that a Mollah, named Chadely, was the first amongst the Arabians who made use of coffee to relieve himself from a continual drowsiness, which hindered him from attending punctually to his nightly devotions. His dervishes did the same, and their example was followed by the lawyers, and others who had no occasion to keep themselves awake, so became a general beverage. That its introduction is of a modern date may be inferred from its not being known to the Romans or Greeks; neither do any of the chroniclers of the Crusades make mention of coffee. It was in use in Persia during the fifteenth century, but during the following century it encountered both political and religious opposition. In Constantinople the public coffee-houses were closed, the Government apprehending they were the receptacles for disaffection. The religious grievance was that the dervishes had discovered that coffee roasted was a kind of coal, and coal being one of the substances interdicted by Mohammed, was therefore declared not good for human food.

It was first introduced in Marseilles in 1644, and in Paris in 1657, by the traveller Thévenot, and from that time the exotic beverage gradually acquired favour. In 1674, an Armenian opened the first coffee-house in Paris. In this country, coffee was first introduced in 1652, by Mr. Edwards, a Turkish merchant; he brought home with him a Greek servant, Pasquil Rosea, who opened the first coffeehouse in England in St. Michael's Alley, Cornhill.

The Dutch were the first to plant the coffee-tree in their colonies, having procured some berries from Mocha, which they sowed with success in Batavia, about 1690.

An interesting narrative is related of the introduction of coffee into the French West Indies. In 1717, several plants were sent to Martinique, under the care of M. de Clieux. The voyage was long and disastrous, and all the plants died but one; and M. de Clieux being, with the rest on board, reduced to a very short allowance of water, divided his share with his solitary plant, and succeeded in getting it safe to

Martinique, where it flourished, and afforded a stock for the neighbouring islands.

Thus, in the course of nearly four centuries, has a berry, which was only used before by a few wandering tribes, become known to the civilized world, taken its place, and become an important article of food.

The finest coffee comes from Aden, and is known as Mocha; the next in repute is from Ceylon and Java; the inferior from South America and the West Indies. A coffee-tree in full vigour will produce from 2 to 3 lbs. of coffee berries. The consumption for the whole world is estimated at 600 millions of pounds.

The French are considered the best makers of this delicious beverage in Europe. The Turks and Arabs boil each cup by itself, and only for a moment. They do not separate the grounds from the infusion, and use neither sugar nor milk.

The excellence of coffee depends much on the roasting. To perform this operation, a drachm of good fresh butter and 2 drachms of sugar put into the cylinder, with the coffee, while roasting, will be found an improvement.

If coffee is insufficiently roasted, it will have little flavour, will lie heavy on the stomach, and probably produce nausea and vomiting. If too much roasted, it becomes acrid, and acquires a disagreeable burnt taste. Properly roasted coffee should have a chocolate brown colour, and look bright and oily. It should be kept air-tight, as it loses its aroma by exposure.

In a medical point of view, coffee will be found to act as an aperient if a glass of cold water be taken immediately before partaking of it. Strong coffee is a powerful stimulant and cordial. In cases of faintness or exhaustion from labour or sickness, coffee is one of the most cordial restoratives we have, promoting digestion and exhilarating the spirits. It allays hunger to a certain extent, and imparts a feeling of comfort to most persons; with some, however, coffee is heavy and difficult of digestion. Difference of temperament produces different effects on coffee-drinkers; but, generally speaking, a prudent use of this beneficial beverage makes it a valuable article of diet: it is also reputed to be an excellent safeguard against gout and gravel. The esteemed properties of coffee are mainly due to the alkaloid caffeine, which is identical in its character to theine, the principle of tea.

Caffric Acid is a peculiar acid contained in raw coffee; *caffeone* a brown aromatic oil, formed during the roasting of coffee. In reference to chicory, that doubtful improver of coffee, we may say that it gives a dark appearance to the liquid, and a bitter flavour, making the coffee appear stronger than it really is, to the deterioration of its flavour.

The use of isinglass or any artificial finings to clarify coffee is objectionable, for the reason that such a process removes much of the astringency and vivacity of the infusion.

A cup of coffee stirred with a pod of vanilla will acquire a delicious flavour.

Ground coffee is frequently adulterated with roasted beans.

Chicory Detected.—When the presence of chicory is suspected, place a teaspoonful of the coffee on the top of a tumbler of cold water; if pure, it will float for some time, and hardly colour the water; but if chicory is present, it will rapidly absorb, and impart a red tint to the water as it falls.

A good liquor for making coffee is made by first infusing a handful of oats in a quart of boiling water for a quarter of an hour; then strain and add them to another quart of water; boil for half an hour, strain clear, and make your coffee with the liquid; it will taste like vanilla coffee.

Clarification, as practised by the Arabs, is to wrap a wet cloth around the pot containing the made coffee; this method is only applicable to an infusion of pure coffee.

A French mode of effecting this is, while the biggin is by the fire, to pour on the top of the liquid half a cup of cold water, which soon clarifies the coffee.

A French method of making coffee is to allow 1 oz. of fresh-ground coffee to nearly half a pint of water; the coffee is put into the upper chamber of the cafètiere, which is previously heated, and the mouth of the spout stopped with a cork; pour in the water, and let it slowly percolate by the side of the fire, with as much heat as it can have without allowing it to boil.

In making coffee in an old-fashioned coffee-pot, put in the coffee first, then pour on the boiling water; pour out a cupful, return it again; repeat this twice, it will soon clear itself; but it must not boil incessantly, for violent boiling will spoil it; keep it closely covered, so as to retain the aroma.

In making coffee, allow, at least, one teaspoonful to each person.

A mode of making coffee is to put ½ lb. fresh-ground coffee in a basin, and to break into it an egg entire, shell and all; and then mix it with a spoon to the consistence of mortar. Place this in a coffee-pot with tepid water, let it boil up and break three times; allow it to stand by the fire, but be careful it does not boil. It will soon come as clear as amber, a deliciously rich drink.

Café au Lait.—Make the coffee with boiling milk, instead of water; sugar to taste.

Café Gloria.—Equal quantities of strong, bright coffee and Cognac; sugar to taste.

Café au Lait.—Pint of good coffee, pint of boiled milk, ¼ pint of boiled cream, 1 drop essence of vanilla; sugar to taste.

Café Noir.—Half-cupful strong, bright coffee, half-cupful Cognac; sugar and vanilla to taste.

Coffee Milk.—Boil a dessert-spoonful of coffee (2 drachms) in a pint of milk for a quarter of an hour; add shavings of isinglass, to clear it; let it boil a few minutes; let it rest and settle clear.

Coffee Ratafia (*Ratafia de Café*).—1 lb. of roasted fresh-ground Mocha coffee; macerate for 10 days in 1 quart of spirit; strain clear, and add 2 pints clarified syrup, and of water 1 quart.

Coffee Ratafia.—1 ½ lb. best roasted and fresh-ground Mocha coffee, 1 ½ lb. pulverized sugar-candy, ½ oz. bruised cinnamon, 2 drachms grated nutmeg, 2 oz. sweet almonds (blanched and bruised), ½ gallon pure rectified spirit; put these ingredients in a jar, and tie it over the mouth with a bladder; boil in a *water bath* for 12 hours, and keep it in a warm place for two days; filter clear; it will be fit for use in one month.

Coffee Granato.—Quart of Mocha coffee, strong and bright; 1 pint of clear syrup; put in a freezing pot; half freeze, and serve.

Liqueur de Café.—To an infusion of good fresh-ground coffee, add 1 quart of water; strain clear to 2 pints strong syrup; add 2 pints rectified spirit.

Coffee Syrup.—1 pint clear, strong-made coffee to 1 pint of syrup; clarify.

Coffee Vanilla.—One pint clear-made coffee, flavoured with vanilla, ¼ pint of Cognac, ¼ pint of syrup.

COCOA AND CHOCOLATE

Cocoa and Chocolate are prepared from the roasted seeds of the *Theobroma Cacoa*. This tree is a native of Mexico, and has been introduced into the West Indies and other tropical parts of the world. The best cocoa comes from Caraccas, Trinidad, and Surinam; there are also other places producing good cocoa. The cocoa-tree is, both in size and shape, similar to a young cherry-tree; the fruit is dispersed on short stalks over the stem and principal branches. The tree bears flowers and fruit simultaneously, and yields two crops of berries annually; these are fit for gathering in June and December; a good bearing tree producing from 20 to 30 pods, which average 20 to 30 nuts, from which the manufacturers produce cocoa or chocolate. The colour of the pods changes from green to yellow when they are gathered. When two pods happen to grow together, one extracts all the nutrition from the other, thriving on its decay. Cocoa and chocolate are prepared from the nuts, by freeing them from the pulp and then making them undergo a process similar to malting;

they are afterwards roasted in a perforated cylinder, and are then freed from their husks and made into cocoa or chocolate, which is similar to cocoa, but made into a paste, and contains sugar, and generally some flavouring addition, as vanilla or other aromatic substance. Chocolate was made in Mexico and other parts long before the discovery of America by Columbus, who brought home some samples; and it has been the favourite beverage of the Spaniards ever since. Cocoa-nibs were used by the Indians as money: 150 nuts were equal to a Spanish real. It is very popular in France and Italy: the French are considered the best makers of chocolate. Genuine chocolate should dissolve in the mouth, without a gritty feeling, leaving a sensation of freshness on the palate.

The Spanish Mode of Soaking Chocolate is to break a portion from the cake and to let it soak eight hours in milk or water; then slowly warming the decoction, to mill it all the time with a notched stick (worked with a piece of string round the handle), passed through a hole in the lid of the pot. The best chocolate is that which dissolves entirely in water, leaving no grounds or sediment at the bottom of the vessel. Chocolate should not be made till required for use; water is better than milk for making chocolate, which should on no account be allowed to boil, as the oil would then pass to the surface; neither coffee nor tea approaches cocoa or chocolate for nutritive properties. The latter contains every ingredient necessary to the sustenance of the body; its active principle is *Theobromine*, an alkaloid which is akin in character to *theine* and *caffeine*, the active principles of tea and coffee.

Cocoa, when unadulterated, forms a wholesome nutritive beverage, superior, as we have said, to tea or coffee, but it is apt to disagree with those unaccustomed to its use, on account of the large quantity of gluten, starch, and fat it contains; in which case an excellent plan is, before partaking of the cocoa or chocolate, to chew well and swallow a dry crust just previous to the cup of cocoa; it has the effect of exciting the saliva. Of the preparations of cocoa, the best descriptions for use are cocoa-nibs, which are simply cocoa-nuts ground. To make cocoa from nibs, place them in a clean coffee-pot by the side of the fire, pour on boiling water, allow the infusion to simmer eight hours, taking care it does not boil (if it does, a coagulum will form which cannot be dissolved by water); then strain clear.

Flake Cocoa: cocoa-nuts crushed between rollers.

Prepared Cocoa is made by grinding the nuts into powder and mixing a soluble substance, easily diffusible in milk or water.

Cocoa or Chocolate is made by rendering it fine, and making it into a paste with a little boiling water, adding the sugar, and pouring in the boiling milk or water with one hand, slowly, while you beat it into a froth with the other; it is then ready for use: it deteriorates by keeping.

Creme de Cacoa.—Infuse 5 oz. Caraccas cocoa-nibs (crushed), 1 pod of vanilla, ¼ oz. of cinnamon, and 1 drop essence of almonds, in 1 quart of brandy, for ten days; strain, press, filter clear; add 1 quart of syrup (clarified).

Chocolate Parfait Amour.—Dissolve ½ lb. vanilla chocolate in sufficient water; in a bottle of brandy, digest 1 oz.

bruised cinnamon, ½ oz. of cloves, and a pinch of salt; in three days, add the chocolate; macerate one week; let it be closely corked; then strain clear.

Chocolate Wine.—Infuse in a bottle of Marsala, or raisin wine, 4 oz. of chocolate, and sugar if required; in three days strain.

ESSENCES, SPICES, ETC., USED IN MAKING CUPS

Angelica contains a volatile oil, which is very useful in flavouring; it is very common in gardens in this country.

Allspice is the immature fruit or berry of the *Eugenia pimenta*—a myrtaceous plant, native of the West Indies. It combines the flavour of nutmegs, cloves, and cinnamon; hence its name. It yields a fine essence, which can be made thus:—Pound some allspice; put it into a 2 oz. phial, which fill up with spirits of wine; digest, and strain.

Essence of Allspice.—To 2 oz. spirits of wine, add 1 drachm oil of nutmeg.

Essence of Aniseed can be made by infusion of the bruised seeds in spirit; or by mixing 1 drachm oil of aniseed with 1 oz. rectified spirit.

Essence of Almonds.—Either macerate bruised bitter almonds in spirit, or mix 2 oz. of spirit with ¼ oz. essential oil of bitter almonds.

Balm (*Melissa officinalis*) is a native of Italy and South of Europe. It has a weak aromatic taste, and lemon-like smell. It was formerly held in great estimation in all complaints appertaining to the nervous system, and was highly recommended in melancholic and hypochondriacal affections. Like borage, however, it has lost its medicinal repute; but an infusion of its leaves is still used as a gentle aromatic and tonic. It makes an agreeable diluent drink in fevers, acidulated with lemon-juice or diluted citric acid. Balm yields an essential oil of a pale yellow colour. It is much used to impart an aromatic taste to beverages.

Borage (*Borage officinalis*) is reputed to be a native of Aleppo. It was formerly much esteemed for supposed medicinal virtues. The old herbalists ranked it as one of the four cardinal flowers; but it has neither smell, warmth, nor pungency. It is an annual plant, of somewhat coarse appearance, with thick stem, containing an insipid viscous juice, which, being subject to heat, forms crystals of nitre. Made into a clarified syrup, it is useful in pectoral affections and disorders requiring a cool treatment. The flowers and upper leaves are very useful in infusing a peculiar cooling taste to summer beverages. It sows its own seed, and comes up without care; and its beautiful blue flowers (which appear from May till October) are very useful in company with those of the nasturtium in decorating salads.

Cinnamon.—This well-known spice is the inner bark of

the *Laurus cinnamomum*, a species of laurel. It is largely cultivated in the Island of Ceylon, especially in the neighbourhood of Colombo. The cinnamon-tree emits no smell while growing, except a little from the blossoms, which are white. The leaves and footstalks are slightly aromatic; but it is the bark alone which gives out that delicious odour, to which no other perfume bears resemblance. Moore's beautiful simile is perfectly true to Nature as regards this tree:—

"The dream of the injured patient mind,
That smiles at the wrongs of men,
Is found in the bruised and wounded rind
Of cinnamon, sweetest then."

The cinnamon bark, before being dried, is of a pale yellow, about the thickness of parchment. The best is rather pliable, and that quality distinguishes it from the inferior kinds, as well as its colour, the commoner being browner and thicker. Owing to the high price of cinnamon, the bark of cassia is much substituted for it; but it is much thicker and coarser than cinnamon, and lacks the peculiar sweet delicious taste of the genuine bark.

Essence of Cinnamon, or Cassia, can be made by infusing the broken spice in a phial, and filling up with spirit; or, to 2 ½ oz. of proof spirit, add 10 drops oil of cinnamon.

Cloves.—This valuable spice is the produce of a tree known to botanists as the *Caryophyllus aromaticus*, or clove-tree, which grows very plentifully in the Island of Amboyna. The cloves of commerce are the unexpanded flower-buds, and are first obtained when the tree is six years old. The preserved fruit is called "mother of cloves," and is a great favourite with the Dutch.

Essence of Cloves can be made by infusion; or, ½ drachm oil of cloves in 2 oz. spirits of wine.

Cucumber (*Cucumis sativus*).—This esculent is chiefly characterized by its cooling and aperient qualities, and, for those who can digest it, it is not unwholesome; it is very useful in imparting a pleasing soft flavour to beverages, if judiciously used.

Essence of Citrons.—Oil of citrons, 30 drops; proof spirit, 1 oz.

Essence of Carraways.—Oil of carraway, ½ drachm; proof spirit, 2 drachms.

Cream of Tartar, or Bitartrate of Potash.—During the fermentation of the grape-juice, or must, a crystallized stony matter, called "argol," is deposited; this consists chiefly of bitartrate of potash, with a little tartrate of lime and other matters, and is the source of all the tartaric acid met with in commerce. The salt in question exists in the juice in considerable quantity; it is, however, sparingly soluble in water, but still less so in dilute alcohol; hence, as the fermentation proceeds, the quantity of spirit increases, and it is then slowly deposited. The acid of the fruit is thus removed as the sugar disappears. It is this circumstance that renders grape-juice alone fit for making good wine; for, when that of gooseberries or currants, &c, is employed as a substitute, the malic and citric acids which these fruits contain cannot be withdrawn. There is no other resource than to add sugar in sufficient quantity to mask and conceal the natural acidity of the liquor.—*Fowndes' Chemistry.*

Guava Jelly is made from the fruit of the guava (*Psidium pysiferum*), which is a native of tropical America; it is most useful in flavouring many drinks, especially Punches.

Ginger is the creeping fleshy root of the *Zingiber officinale*, a native of the Indies. The appearance of the plant is similar to the lily of the valley, growing about two feet high; its cultivation is very easy, the root being taken up when the stems are withered and scaled in order to kill it, and afterwards dried in the sun. Of the different varieties, the best is that known as unbleached Jamaica, which is large and fleshy. That imported from the East Indies is stronger than the Jamaica. Ginger is less pungent than might be expected, judging from its effects on the organs of taste. The syrup of the delicious preserved green ginger is very useful as a liquor, and for flavouring purposes. The qualities of ginger depend very much on a pale yellow volatile oil, lighter than water, called oil of ginger (*Oleum zingiberis*). The essence can be made by grating 6 oz. fine ginger, 1 oz. lemon-peel; put in a bottle, adding sufficient spirits of wine, or 2 oz. ginger grated, ¼ pint spirits of wine, and 1 drop of essence of cayenne.

Essence of Jargonelle Pear.—Pear oil (acetate of oxide of amyl), ¼ fluid oz.; rectified spirit, 2 oz.

Essence of Apple.—Apple oil (valerianate of oxide of amyle), ¼ fluid oz.; rectified spirit, 2 oz.

Lemon-Juice (Succhus limonum).—The juice of this valuable fruit is too well known to need any introduction, while its wholesome character is also firmly established. It is the best known remedy in scurvy, being used in large quantities in the navy for that purpose; it is also much used in other "ills that flesh is heir to." Lemon-juice is very liable to spoil, if long exposed to the air; it is, therefore, mixed with about one-tenth of its weight in brandy. The best lemons come from Messina, and the South of Europe.

Oil of Lemons is obtained by the thin peel, placed in hair bags and subjected to a great pressure, 100 lemons producing 2 oz. of oil.

Citric Acid is obtained in large quantities from the juice of the lemon and the genus *Citrus*. It is much used as a substitute for lemon-juice, it being the cause of the grateful acidity of the lemon, citron, &c.

Essence of Lemons.—Fresh lemon-peel, ½ lb.; spirits of wine, 1 pint; oil of lemons, 1 drachm; digest, strain, press, and filter.

Lemon-scented Verbena (*Aloysia citriodora*) is much used as a substitute for balm in cups; its peculiar lemon-like flavour and smell are much appreciated in light-wine drinks.

Essence of Lemon-Grass Oil.—Lemon-grass oil, ½ fluid drachm, put into 2 oz. of pure spirit.

Nutmeg is the shelled seed of the *Myristica moschata*, a tree which grows principally in the Isles of Banda. The nutmeg-tree is like a pear-tree in shape and form, with a laurel-like leaf, which, when bruised, emits an aromatic perfume. The flowers are small, and have no smell. The fruit is similar to a walnut in form, but more fleshy, and full of juice. The external pulp dries up to a crust of a deep red colour, that, on opening at one side, discloses a membranous coat of a beautiful red tint, known to us as mace, which lies immediately over the thin and brittle shell of the nutmeg.

The young nutmegs are preserved in vinegar and sugar.

A nutmeg-tree will yield three crops annually, the tree bearing fruit and blossoms at the same time.

Essence of Nutmeg.—Grate a nutmeg; put it in a phial; fill up with spirit; digest and strain; or add ½ drachm oil of nutmeg to 1 oz. of spirits of wine.

Orange (Citrus aurantium), of which there are two species, the sweet and bitter. It is the best known and wholesomest of all subacid fruits; it contains less citric acid than the lemon. The bitter or Seville orange (*Citrus bigaradia*) is very useful, both to the liquorist and as an ingredient in medicine. The peel of orange is more warm and grateful than that of lemon, containing more volatile oil.

Neroli is the essential oil of the orange flower. It is very powerful, and lighter than water, in which it is soluble.

Bergamot (Citrus bergamia).—The rind of this kind of orange produces the well-known oil of bergamot; it is very powerful. The fruit is smooth, of a pale yellow colour. 100 oranges will yield 2 ½ oz. essential oil of bergamot.

Essence of Orange-peel.—Peel ½ dozen of either Seville, Tangerine, or sweet oranges, very thin; add ½ pint spirits of wine; digest ten days, then add ½ pint good pale sherry; in 12 or more days strain with pressure and filter clear.

Pine-apple.—This most useful and richly-flavoured esculent is the fruit of the *Anana sassativa*, a native of the West Indies and the tropics. It is imported from thence to this country in great quantities. The very best pines are grown artificially in this country. It is an astringent, and is of great use for its exquisite flavour.

Essence of Pine-apple.—Pine-apple oil (butyric ether), ½ oz.; rectified spirit, 3 ½ oz.

Essence of Spruce.—Boil in water the young tops of the black spruce-fir (*Abies nigra*), and concentrate the decoction by evaporation.

Essence of Spruce.—A decoction prepared from the young tops of the *Pinus larix*, boiled till it evaporates to a thick syrup; this, fermented with molasses, makes spruce beer.

Essence of Violets.—2 fluid drachms orris root oil; rectified spirit, 5 oz.

PART II

Cups, and Social Drinks

CUPS

The words "cup" and "bumper" and many other of our social terms, can be traced to the convivial usages of the ancients. The custom of dedicating a cup to a favourite deity led, by an easy transition, to that of pledging each other—the origin of modern toasts. According to Casaubon, the ancients took three cups at their banquets: one, to allay thirst; another, for pleasure; and a third, as a libation to Jupiter Servator:

"Ho! boy, there, a cup! Brim full to the new moon.
Ho! boy, there, a cup! Brim full for the midnight.
Ho! boy, there, a cup! Brim full to the health
Of him we would honour, Murena the Augur."

                                        HORACE.

The duty of serving the wine amongst the ancient Romans was given to boys—slaves, who were well dressed—the wine being kept in large earthen vases, into which the cyanthus (or goblet) was adroitly dipped when it required replenishing.

The cyanthus contained about as much as our modern wine-glass, or else how could they say—

> "Let our bumpers, while jovial we give out the toast
> In gay compotations, be ten at the most:
> The ninth to the Muses in order must follow,
> The tenth a libation be made to Apollo?"

It was also of sufficient capacity to give rise to the phrase, "To get into one's cups," which originated with the Romans. Pisander mentions that Hercules crossed the ocean in his cup, which may have handed down the phrase, "half seas over," in this sense.

> "How you totter, good feet! Have a care of my
>   bones!
> If you fail me, I pass all the night on these
>   stones."

The "Cup of Hercules"—which was drunk off and caused the death of Alexander the Great—contained nearly four English quarts. "Here," says Seneca, "is this hero, unconquered by all the toils of prodigious marches, by the dangers of sieges and combats, by the most violent extremes of heat and cold—here he lies, subdued by intemperance, and struck to the earth."

The *ampulla* (or vessel for carrying the wine) was covered with leather, and may justly claim to be the original "leathern bottel."

> "I wish that his soul in heaven may dwell
> "Who first invented the leathern bottel."

These "bottels" were very different affairs to the tankards of leather known as "Black Jacks," one or more of which are still preserved at the Hospital of the Holy Cross, near Winchester. The origin of the term "bumper" is ascribed to the French phrase "*bon père*," or boon companion.

"If it be true, good wine needs no bush." The derivation of this term is owing to the ancient custom of the Romans hanging a branch of ivy, a plant sacred to Bacchus, over the wine-shop door, and hence their proverb, "Vendible wine needs no ivy hung up." This custom has been adopted in many wine countries.

Bosky, or *boosy*, is undoubtedly an allusion to a familiar acquaintance with the friendly shade of the bush, where, "in his cup, the boosy poet sings."

Pegging away is derived from the peg tankard which held 2 quarts of ale, studded with a row of 8 pins at equal distances, so as to allow a ½ pint between each pin; hence the phrase, also, of a man in his cups being a peg higher or lower.

Hob-nob is now an euphemism for an invitation to a social bout. It is found in Shakespeare's "Twelfth Night:" "Hob-nob is his word: give't or take't."

The Stirrup Cup, once so honoured an institution amongst us, has its origin in the parting cup of the ancients.

The Loving Cup is a splendid feature of the Hall feasts of the City and Inns of Court. The cup is of silver or silver-gilt, and is filled with spiced wine, immemorially termed "sack." "Immediately after the dinner and grace, the Master and Wardens drink to their visitors a hearty welcome; the cup is then passed round the table, and each guest, after he has drunk, applies his napkin to the mouth of the cup before he passes it to his neighbour. The more formal practice is for the person who pledges with the loving cup to stand up and bow to his neighbour, who, also standing, removes the cover with his right hand, and holds it while the other drinks; a custom said to have originated in the precaution to keep the right, or dagger-hand, employed, that the person who drinks may be assured of no treachery, like that practised by Elfrida on the unsuspecting King Edward the Martyr at Corfe Castle, who was slain while drinking. This was why the loving cup possessed a cover."—*F. W. Fairholt.*

"You may pay too dear for your whistle," evidently originated with the whistle brought to Scotland by a Danish gentleman in the train of Queen Anne of Denmark, with which he challenged all Scottish bacchanalians to compete with him in powers of drinking. He who could at the termination of the drinking bout blow the whistle, was to keep it as a trophy of his powers as a worthy champion of Bacchus. After making many exclaim with Silenus—

> "Innumerable pains I now endure
> Through thee, O Bacchus!"

he was encountered and worsted by Sir Robert Lawrie, of Maxwelton, who, after three days and nights' contest, left his Scandinavian antagonist under the table,

"And blew on the whistle his requiem shrill."

It is on the contest for this whistle that Burns founded the ballad of "The Whistle"—

"I sing of a Whistle, a Whistle of worth;
I sing of a Whistle, the pride of the North,
Was brought to the Court of our good Scottish
    King,
And long with this Whistle all Scotland shall
    ring."

"If you want any more you must whistle for it," came from a vessel having a whistle attached to it, which was blown when it required replenishing: it was called the "whistle tankard."

"Your health!" or "Health be to you!" the salutation of our forefathers on occasion of drinking to each other, it is said, originated in this wise:—On the first interview between Vortigern and Rowena, the daughter of Hengist, she presented a cup of wine to him kneeling, saying, "Hlaford Kyning, waes-hael!" *i.e.* "Lord King, health be to you!" The king, being unacquainted with the Saxon language, asked the meaning, and being told, and also to answer by saying, "Drinc-hae!" he did so, and kissed the damsel, and pledged her. The custom long remained in England of pledging each other. The one who drank said, "Was-hael," and the recipient of the cup said, "Drinc-hael." Wassail songs and the wassail bowl were amongst the most noted of the Christmas festivities. The wassail songs were sung generally by strolling minstrels, and hence may be traced our present waits and carol singers.

Among the Scandinavian barbarians, the highest point of felicity which they hoped to obtain in their future state was to drink mead and ale in the Hall of Odin, out of the skulls of those they had overpowered, and get intoxicated while listening to the music of a shin-bone made into a pipe. There is no lack of examples of the custom being continued for a long time, and being adopted by other nations than those mentioned. Mandeville relates that the old Guebres exposed the dead bodies of their parents to the fowls of the air, reserving only the skulls, of which he says, "The son maketh a cuppe, and therefrom drynkethe he with gret devocion." Warnefrid tells us "Albin slew Cuminum, and converted his head into a drinking vessel." In our age, Lord Byron had a skull mounted into a carousing cup, and wrote this Bacchanalian inscription on it,—

"Start not, nor deem my spirit fled:
In me behold the only skull
From which, unlike a living head,
Whatever flows is never dull.

I lived, I loved, I quaff'd like thee:
I died: let earth my bones resign:
Fill up—thou canst not injure me,
The worm hath fouler lips than thine.

Better to hold the sparkling grape
Than nurse the earthworm's slimy brood;
And circle in the goblet's shape
The drink of gods, than reptiles' food.

Where once my wit, perchance, hath shone,
In aid of others' let me shine;
And when, alas! our brains are gone,
"What nobler substitute than wine?

Quaff while thou canst, another race,
When thou and thine, like me, are sped,
May rescue thee from earth's embrace,
And rhyme and revel with the dead.

Why not? since through life's little day
Our heads such sad effects produce?
Redeem'd from worms and wasting clay,
This chance is theirs—to be of use."

The wits and beauties of the Court of Charles the Second were partial to a toast in their drinks, and pledging each, or toasting each other; it was also a point of gallantry for a beau to drink as many cups as there were letters in the name of the lady who was toasted, which was similar to the old Romish custom of drinking the health of their Emperor; for instance, that of Germanicus was celebrated with ten, and Caesar with six, and so on. Another usage at the feasts of ancient Greece and Rome, was to drink the health of absent friends; it was a proof of the esteem of the one whose health was drunk by the number of cups emptied in their honour. The Jacobite mode of drinking the Pretender's health was by first placing a bowl of water on the table, and then giving the usual toast, "The King!" which meant "over the water."

Hot compound drinks continued to be in vogue till a recent date. This taste is said to have originated with the Romans, with whom mixed potations were quite a passion, their favourite resort being the house of warm drinks,— places not unlike our coffee and public houses.

WINE CUPS

"O, Peggy, Peggy, when thou go'st to brew,
Consider well what you're about to do,
Be very wise—very sedately think
That what you're going to make is—drink!
Consider who must drink that drink, and then
What 'tis to have the praise of honest men;
The future ages shall of Peggy tell,
The nymph who spiced the brewages so well."

Claret Cup à la Brunow, for a Party of Twenty.—This cup is much appreciated in Russia, and has long enjoyed deserved popularity amongst the highest in that country.

Put into a large vessel imbedded in a mixture of ice and salt—the proportion of 3 lbs. of salt to 12 lbs. of ice is a very good one—some sprigs of balm and borage, or slices of cucumber (not too much, or it will render the drink disagreeably over-herbed); pour on the herbs 1 pint of sherry, ½ pint of brandy; then the peel of a lemon rubbed off lightly, with a lump of sugar (oleo-saccharum);* add the strained juice of 1 lemon and 3 oranges, ½ pint of Curaçoa, 1 gill of ratafia of raspberries, 2 bottles of German seltzer water, 3 bottles of soda, and 3 bottles of claret; sweeten to taste; draw the "herbing," and serve. It can be made with champagne or any sparkling wine, by substituting some other liqueur; for instance, in the case of champagne, use noyeau instead of ratafia of raspberries.

Claret Cup à la Webber.—Bruise 1 doz. of cloves, ½ doz. allspice, which digest in 1 gill of sherry, and ½ gill of pale brandy; in three hours strain, and prepare the oleo-saccharum of 2 lemons.

Into a vessel (imbedded in ice) put a few young borage leaves and a sprig of verbena (*Aloysia citriodora*); pour on the spirit and a liqueur-glassful of noyeau, Curaçoa, or Maraschino; add ¼ lb. pounded sugar, the oleo-saccharum and juice (strained) of 3 lemons, 3 bottles of claret; sweeten to taste; withdraw the herbing; add 1 bottle champagne, 2 bottles of soda-water, 1 ½ pint lumps of ice; cover close; serve as soon as possible.

Claret Cup for a Large Out-Door Gathering.—In a small jug put some slices of cucumber, peeled; one or two drops of lemon-grass oil (*citronelle*) on sugar (or some bruised

---

* Oleo-saccharum is the name by which the sugared essence of lemon and orange peel, &c, is known. It is made by rubbing a piece of sugar on the outer rind of the fruit, and scraping it as it absorbs the essential oil. To save much repetition, this term will be used throughout the world for this latter process.

balm leaves), 2 drops oil of orange-peel on sugar, 10 drops essence of lemon, 1 drop neroli; cover these ingredients with brandy; let them digest for four or five hours, then strain with pressure; bottle the mixture, and add whatever other flavour might be desired—this forming the flavouring basis.

When the cup is required, mix together 6 bottles *vin ordinaire*, 2 bottles of Roussillon, 1 bottle Rota Tent, 1 bottle raisin wine, ½ gill raspberry syrup, ½ gill violet syrup (or green ginger ditto), or 1 pint of Curaçoa, and 3 bottles of sparkling cider; sweeten and flavour according to taste, ice up, and just before serving add 5 bottles aërated lemonade, and 8 bottles of potash water, 2 of seltzer water, and some lumps of Lake ice in the cup: lumps or shaven ice can be used in the tumblers used for drinking.

Balaklava Nectar Claret Cup, à la Soyer, for a Party of Fifteen.—Put the thin paring of a lemon into a punch bowl; add 2 tablespoonfuls of crushed sugar, the juice of 2 lemons (strained), slices of cucumber, with the peel on; add 2 bottles of soda-water, 2 bottles of claret, 1 of champagne; stir up, and serve.

Claret Cup à la Wilberforce.—2 bottles of claret, 1 of sparkling champagne, wine-glass of Maraschino or citronelle; borage, balm, and sugar to the flavour required; ice well, and before serving add 2 bottles seltzer water.

Cambridge Claret Cup.—1 bottle of claret, ½ bottle of sherry, gill of port, gill of cherry-brandy, oleo-saccharum, and strained juice of 1 lemon; sweeten to taste; add cucumber and verbena sufficient to flavour; strain, ice up. When ready for use, add 3 bottles of iced German seltzer water.

Oxford Claret Cup.—2 bottles of claret, pint of dry sherry, ½ gill of brandy, 1 bottle of champagne (iced), ½ gill of noyeau; infuse some young borage and balm leaves in the sherry; when sufficiently herbed, strain; add this to the claret, sweeten to taste, add the noyeau and spirit, ice up; just before serving, add 2 bottles of iced potash water, 1 pint of shaven ice, and the champagne; serve immediately.

Claret Cup à la Lord Saltoun.—Peel 1 lemon fine, cover with pounded sugar, pour over a glass of sherry; add 1 bottle of claret, sprig of verbena, and bottle of soda-water.

Claret Cup à la Stockdale.—2 bottles of claret, 1 bottle of dry Roussillon, ½ gill of cherry-brandy or Kirschwasser; when sufficiently herbed with balm and borage (or cucumber and verbena), strain; sweeten to taste; ice up, add 2 bottles of lemonade, and 1 of German seltzer water.

Claret Cup à la Cutler.—The oleo-saccharum and strained juice of 1 lemon, and 1 Seville orange, infused in 1 bottle of green ginger wine; add a few slices of cucumber, and strain; add 1 bottle of dry Roussillon and 2 bottles of claret; sweeten to taste; ice up, and add 4 bottles of soda-water.

Claret Cup à la Maclean.—Bottle of claret, liqueur-glass of Curaçoa or Maraschino, juice of 1 lemon, oleo-saccharum of ½ lemon, slice of cucumber, and sprig of verbena; strain, ice up, and add 1 or 2 bottles of soda-water.

Claret Cup à la Guy.—Bottle of claret, bottle of sparkling Moselle; add to the above oleo-saccharum and juice of ½ a Seville orange; slice of cucumber; sweeten to taste; ice up, add 1 pint of shaven ice, and 1 bottle of seltzer water.

Claret Cup à la Knott.—2 bottles of claret, ½ pint of orange brandy, ½ gill Curaçao a, slice of cucumber; ice up, and add 3 bottles aërated lemonade.

Claret Cup à la Keble.—Bottle of claret, ½ a pint of raisin or rhubarb wine, ½ gill of pale brandy, 2 or 3 sprigs of young mint; sweeten to taste and strain; add 1 bottle of soda-water, and 1 ½ pint of shaven ice.

Claret Cup à la Gardner.—Take equal proportions of the following spices in powder, sufficient to fill a teaspoonful, cinnamon, cloves, cardamoms, allspice; add to this mixture 1 gill of pale brandy; add the oleo-saccharum of a lemon, the strained juice of 1 lemon and 2 oranges, then add 2 bottles of claret; mix all well together; put in ice; in one hour strain clear; add a thin slice of cucumber, and, just before serving, 2 bottles of soda-water.

Claret Cup.—Bottle of claret, sweetened to taste, and a bottle of iced soda-water.

Claret Cup à la Rawlings.—Bottle of claret, bottles of Rawlings' ginger beer.

Claret Cup à la Jeanes.—2 bottles of good claret, 1 gill of raspberry-water ice, ½ teaspoonful of violet syrup, 1 gill pale brandy; ice up; then mix and add 2 bottles of potash water.

Hot Claret Cup.—2 bottles of claret, 6 drops of essence of ginger, ½ gill ginger syrup, 1 quart of boiling water.

Badminton Cup à la Morrey.—Bottle of claret, bottle of soda-water; sugar to taste; balm and borage; ice up; but do not let the herbs remain in long.

No. 2.—Into a large jug put a few sprigs of balm and

borage, with thin lemon-peel; add ½ gill of brandy, ½ gill of port wine, 2 oz. pounded sugar; pour in 2 bottles of soda-water and claret; stand in refrigerator on ice till required; do not let the herbs or lemon remain in too long, or they will overpower the wine disagreeably.

Burgundy Cup, No. 1.—To 2 bottles of Burgundy add 1 pint of port wine, a gill of good cherry-brandy, juice of 2 oranges and 1 lemon (strained), slice of cucumber, sprig of lemon-scented verbena; mix together half an hour in a refrigerator; withdraw the herbing; add sugar to taste, 3 bottles of seltzer water, and a quart of shaven ice, or lumps.

Burgundy Cup, No. 2.—Bottle of sparkling Burgundy, 1 bottle of Chablis, liqueur-glass of citronelle or Chartreuse, a slice of cucumber, 2 bottles of potash water, and a quart of Lake ice in lumps; then proceed as in previous formula.

Burgundy Cup, No. 3.—Bottle of ordinary Burgundy, ½ gill of ordinary brandy; 4 fresh black-currant leaves or buds, steeped in the brandy two hours; sweeten with 1 oz. powdered sugar-candy; when all well blended, strain the leaves; add bottle of aërated lemonade, and, just before serving, a pound of ice, in small lumps.

Burgundy Cup, No. 4.—Bottle of Burgundy, pint of dry Roussillon; balm and borage, just sufficient to impart a cool aromatic taste; juice of 1 lemon; ½ rind of same, rubbed on sugar; ice up; add 2 bottles of soda-water, and serve without delay. If desired, a little liqueur, either Maraschino, noyeau, or citronelle, will vary the flavour.

Burgundy Cup à la Orbell.—Peel and juice of 2 lemons; quart of seltzer water; 2 bottles of Burgundy; sugar to taste;

when well iced, draw out the peel and serve.

Burgundy Cup à la Guy.—Bottle of sparkling Burgundy, iced; bottle of sparkling Moselle, iced; slice of cucumber; bottle of seltzer water, iced; pint of shaven ice; mix together; serve as soon as required.

Crimean Cup à la Marmora (from Soyer), for a Party of Thirty.—Put 1 quart of syrup of orgeat, 1 pint Cognac brandy, ½ pint Maraschino, ¼ pint Jamaica rum, 3 bottles of champagne, 2 bottles soda-water, 3 ounces sugar, the oleo-saccharum and juice of 4 good lemons, in a vessel; add 2 bottles of soda-water, and stir well till the sugar is dissolved; pour in the syrup of orgeat, and whip the mixture up well with an egg-whisk, in order to whiten the composition; then add the brandy, rum, and Maraschino; strain the whole into the punch-bowl, and, just before serving, add the champagne; stir well with the ladle: this will render the cup creamy and mellow.

Champagne Cup à la Brunow, vide *Claret* No. 1.

Crimean Cup à la Wyndham, No. 3 (*for a Party of Five*).—The oleo-saccharum of ½ orange; add 1 large wine-glass of Maraschino, half one of Curaçoa, half one of Cognac; mix well together; pour in 2 bottles of soda-water, 1 of champagne; mix well with the spoon; add 1 lb. lump of Lake ice.

Champagne Cup à la Ariadne, No. 4.—Bottle of champagne (iced); gill of Amontillado; liqueur-glass of citronelle or Maraschino; juice and paring of a Seville orange or lemon, rubbed on sugar; verbena and cucumber; sugar to taste; bottle of seltzer water.

Champagne Cup à la Parisienne, No. 5.—Bottle of sparkling

champagne (iced); bottle dry ditto (iced); a teaspoonful of absinthe Suisse; syrup to taste; mix the syrup and liqueur together well; add the dry champagne; quart of shaven ice, and immediately before serving pour in the bottle of sparkling champagne; soda or seltzer if desired.

Champagne Cup à la Tanfield.—Bottle of sparkling champagne (iced); bottle of Chablis (iced); liqueur-glass of Chartreuse, or eau de Dantzic; slice of cucumber or of borage; 2 bottles of potass water or seltzer (iced); 1 pint of shaven ice.

Champagne Cup, No. 7.—Bottle of champagne, 1 pint of tea, gill of pale brandy, or Curaçoa; make an infusion of 1 oz. of gunpowder and orange Pekoe tea, mixed, but be careful not to let it stand too long, or it will be unpleasantly strong and bitter; filter the decoction clear, to which add the brandy, and sweeten to taste; ice up, and add the champagne just before serving.

Champagne Cup, No. 8.—Bottle of sparkling champagne (iced), bottle of soda-water (iced), 2 oz. powdered loaf-sugar, sprig of borage and balm, juice and thin peel of 1 lemon; pour the champagne on the lemon, sugar, and herbs; cover the vessel, which is in ice, till the sugar is dissolved; add the soda-water.

Champagne Cup, No. 9.—1 bottle sparkling champagne (iced), liqueur-glass of Curaçoa or Maraschino, liqueur-glass of pale brandy, sprig of verbena, thin slice of cucumber, 2 bottles of potash water; ice as before stated.

Champagne Cup, No. 10.—1 bottle of sparkling champagne, 3 bottles of green-gooseberry wine, ½ pint of orange-brandy; sugar to taste; 6 bottles of aërated lemonade, or soda-water;

slice of cucumber, 1 drop essence of lemon on sugar; put
these ingredients in a jug, with large lump of ice; immediately before serving, add the champagne.

Champagne Cup, No. 11.—2 bottles of sparkling champagne
(well iced), ½ pint of strawberry or lemon water ice, 2
bottles of soda-water (iced); mix and use immediately.

Champagne or Rhenish Wine Cup.—2 bottles of sparkling
champagne, or Rhenish (iced), 1 pint of milk punch
(iced), 1 pint of shaven ice, 3 bottles of soda-water (iced);
pour into a vessel, in ice, these ingredients; cover this for
a quarter of an hour, and serve.

Asmannshausen Cup, No. 1.—1 bottle of Asmannshausen,
bottle of sparkling Moselle (iced), 2 bottles of German
seltzer water; if a liqueur is desired, add liqueur-glass of
Creme de Rose; pour the hock (with the liqueur, if used
together) into a cool vessel; add the seltzer water and
Moselle; drop in a large lump of ice; stir, and serve.

Heidelberg Cup, No. 2.—1 bottle of red Rhenish wine,
liqueur-glass of Kirschwasser or cherry-brandy, strained
juice of a lemon, half a rind of same rubbed on sugar,
pounded loaf sugar to taste, 6 coriander seeds, bruised
with a little pounded cinnamon and steeped in the
liqueur till well flavoured; mix well together and strain;
pour into a jug containing a good lump of ice; then add a
thin slice of cucumber, if a cool taste is desired.

May Trank, a popular Rhine Beverage, No. 3.—Bottle of hock,
2 oz. pounded sugar-candy, juice of 1 orange (or lemon)
strained, 1 dozen woodruff leaves, bruised; put the leaves
in a cool vessel; add the sugar and wine, and, in a few
minutes, the orange-juice.

N.B.—Be careful that the woodruff* does not overpower.

No. 4.—Bottle of sparkling Rhenish, liqueur-glass of pine-apple or ginger syrup, bottle of aërated lemonade (iced), bottle of orangeade (iced) or two bottles of potass water; slice of cucumber; mix the wine and syrup; add the cucumber, and ice up as desired; just before serving add the aërated beverages.

No. 5.—Bottle of Rhenish wine, gill of dry sherry, strained juice and the rind of 1 lemon rubbed on sugar, with slice of cucumber; mix, sweeten to taste, ice up, and before serving add 1 bottle German seltzer water.

No. 6.—Quart of Rhenish wine, ½ a gill of East India arrack, strained juice of 2 lemons, oleo-saccharum of same, 6 woodruff leaves, or sprigs of mint, then mix together; when sufficiently herbed, strain; sweeten to taste; ice up, and, before serving, add 2 bottles of potash water.

No. 7.—Bottle of sparkling hock, sprig of fresh mint, glass of English gin or Scotch whisky; macerate the mint in the spirit till well flavoured; strain, then add 1 pint of shaven ice, and the wine; stir up, and serve.

À la Gurton, No. 8.—Rub the rind of a mandarin orange with a lump of sugar; put this into a jug; 1 drop of lemon-grass oil on sugar and a slice of cucumber; pour on 1 gill of pale brandy; when sufficiently flavoured, strain into a bottle.

---

* Woodruff, on the Rhine called "Wald-meister," is found in woods, round the stems of oaks. It grows about seven inches high, bearing a white jessamine flower. Its perfume is similar to new-mown hay. It keeps its flavour when dried; and it is best to bruise the leaves when required for use. It can be procured at any of the herbalists in Covent Garden.

Take ¼ pint of lemon-juice, strained clear by filtering it through washed sand, which well sweeten; ice well 3 bottles of sparkling hock and 2 bottles of seltzer water; when ready for use, mix the wine and juice together, add ½ gill of citronelle (or Maraschino); and according to taste, the aromatic spirit, then the seltzer water; keep it cool, and serve.

No. 9.—Macerate ½ lb. of fresh greengages, apricots, or peaches in 1 pint of gin; strain with pressure; add this to a quart of Rhenish wine and 1 bottle of potash water. One or more of the kernels bruised and left in the spirit is an improvement.

Bottled Velvet (a la Sir John Bayley).—Bottle of Moselle, ½ pint of dry sherry, thin peel of 1 lemon, 2 tablespoonfuls of pounded sugar; mix when sufficiently flavoured, and strain; add ice, and serve up.

Moselle, No. 2.—Bottle of sparkling Moselle (iced), pint of lemon-water ice; add, if desired, 2 drops of elder-flower water, as it imparts a distinctive flavour; 1 bottle of German seltzer water (iced).

Moselle, No. 3.—Bottle of Moselle (iced), pint of Chablis (iced), ¼ pint of pine-apple ice, bottle of aërated lemonade (iced), bottle of potass water (iced); mix well in iced vessel; serve and add cucumber, if cool taste is required.

Moselle, No. 4.—2 bottles of Moselle (sparkling muscat), ½ gill of pale brandy, ½ pint of thin bright strawberry syrup; mix, and add 1 quart of shaven ice.

Moselle, No. 5.—Infuse in a gill of sherry or brandy (or both) 2 leaves of black currant, 2 leaves of mint, 1 of horehound; when sufficiently herbed, strain clear with pressure; add thin peel of a lemon, the juice of same, and of 2 oranges; put all into a jug with a 2 lb. lump of ice; add a bottle of soda-water and a bottle of sparkling Moselle; stir, cover, and serve.

Moselle, No. 6.—Bottle of Moselle (iced); flavour with Angelique, or a tablespoonful of Crème d'Angelique, bottle of aërated lemonade (iced), or potass water.

Moselle, No. 7.—Bottle of Moselle, wine-glass of dry sherry, 3 slices of pine-apple, or 2 apricots sliced, thin peel of ½ an orange; sugar to taste; bottle of seltzer water, some lumps of Lake ice.

Sauterne.—Bottle of Sauterne, 2 sliced peaches, 1 sliced apricot; infuse the first in sufficient brandy to cover them; strain with pressure; break the stones of the fruit; add to the spirit, and strain; add the wine and 2 bottles of potass water; serve with lumps of Lake ice.

No. 2.—Bottle of Sauterne, wine-glass of Amontillado, 1 drop essence ambergris, on lump of sugar, which break in two, and use half the quantity (ambergris being very powerful); 1 oz. white bruised sugar-candy; mix the sugar, sherry, and ambergris; when well mixed, put in slice of cucumber, the Sauterne, and ice up; add, when ready to serve, bottle of seltzer water.

No. 3.—Bottle of Sauterne, liqueur-glass of citronelle or Maraschino, bottle of potass water, balm and borage; juice of 1 lemon.

No. 4.—2 bottles Sauterne, 1 bottle sparkling muscat Moselle (iced), slice of cucumber, juice of 4 oranges and 2 lemons (strained clear), 3 bottles of potass water (iced); mix all together in a cool jug; serve as cool as possible.

No. 5.—Bottle of Sauterne; bottle of German seltzer water, slice of cucumber, tablespoonful of pounded sugar.

Chablis Cup à la Goodrich.—Dissolve 5 lumps of sugar in a pint of boiling water; add a little thin lemon-peel; when cool, add wine-glass of dry sherry and bottle of Chablis, and a 1 lb. lump of ice.

No. 2.—Put a bottle of Chablis and a liqueur-glass of Chartreuse, Maraschino, or noyeau, into a jug imbedded in ice; add a lump of Lake ice; immediately before serving add the seltzer water.

No. 3.—2 bottles of Chablis, 1 bottle of Sillery Champagne, 1 ditto of aërated lemonade or potass water, slice of cucumber, quart of shaven ice; put all together in a jug which has been some time imbedded in ice; serve as soon as possible.

Sherry Cup à la W. T.—2 bottles dry sherry, 2 bottles aërated lemonade, 1 bottle of potass water, 1 drop of ambergris, on sugar (split the lump of sugar, and only use half of it); balm and borage, as required; sugar to taste; dissolve the ambergris and sugar in 1 bottle of sherry; then the herbing; when flavoured, strain; add the other bottle of sherry on a large lump of ice, in jug; when well cooled, add lemonade and potass; stir and serve.

No. 2, *à la Kenyon.*—2 bottles pale dry sherry, ½ pint Paxaretta wine, juice of 1 lemon, tablespoonful of noyeau, 3 bottles of soda-water; when ready to serve, add 1 quart of shaven ice.

No. 3.—1 bottle of brown sherry, sprig of balm with borage; steep the herbs in the wine, and when flavoured, withdraw it (sherry soon extracts the flavour); add some lumps of ice and 2 bottles Rawlings' ginger beer (iced); this is for immediate use.

No. 4, *à la John Day.*—2 bottles of sherry, ½ pint of Cognac, ¼ pint of Curaçoa; 3 drops essence of almonds; if liked, 2 drops essence of lemons; mix well together; add slice of cucumber, and 2 quarts of shaven ice; or, after well icing, 3 or 4 bottles of soda-water.

No. 5.—2 bottles of brown sherry, ½ pint of Scotch whisky, ½ gill of preserved ginger or pine-apple; put these into a cooler; add slice of cucumber, and, when required, 2 bottles of seltzer water (iced), 2 pints of shaven ice.

No. 6.—2 bottles of sherry, pint lemon-water ice, ½ pint orange-brandy, 2 bottles aërated lemonade (iced), German seltzer water, 3 lumps of sugar (rubbed with lemon-peel), slice of cucumber; add wine, ice, brandy, sugar, cucumber, together; ice up when ready to serve; add lemonade and seltzer.

No. 7.—Bottle of sherry, 1 bottle of sparkling green gooseberry, wine-glass of Kirschwasser, 2 bottles of potash water, quart of shaven ice.

No. 8.—Bottle of sherry, 2 bottles of seltzer or potass water (iced), sprig of mint.

No. 9.—Bottle of dry sherry, ¼ Seville orange-peel, liqueur-glass of Kirschwasser.

No. 10.—Bottle of sherry, 2 bottles of ginger beer.

No. 11.—Bottle of sherry, liqueur-glass essence of punch or shrub, quart of shaven ice, bottle of lemonade or soda-water.

Port-wine Cup.—Bottle of port; ditto of dry Roussillon or Bordeaux wine; a few black-currant tops, steeped in the port wine till they just impart a flavour, or a very small quantity of balm and borage; herb the wine sufficiently to taste, and strain; mix and ice up; sweeten to taste; add 2 bottles seltzer water, and serve.

No. 2.—Bottle of port wine; pint of cold bishop (*vide* page 153), gill of Curaçoa, 2 bottles of seltzer water, 1 pint of shaven ice.

No. 3.—Warm ½ pint of port wine with 2 oz. of sugar, add a little spice to taste; strain clear; when cold, add bottle of soda-water. This is delicious and refreshing.

Cider Cup à la Ensor.—2 bottles of sparkling cider, ½ gill of Curaçoa, ½ gill of brown brandy, ¼ lb. of sugar-candy; the juice strained, and the peel of 1 lemon rubbed on sugar; slice of cucumber; pour ½ pint boiling water on the candy when dissolved and cool; add the brandy, cucumber, liqueur, and juice; in a few minutes, add the cider and a quart of shaven ice; use immediately.

No. 2.—Bottle of sparkling cider, bottle of sparkling perry, pint of Chablis wine, liqueur-glass of citronelle or Maraschino, slice of cucumber, 2 bottles of potass water, pint of pounded ice; mix well; withdraw the cucumber, and serve.

No. 3.—Bottle of cider, gill of dry sherry, slice of pine-apple, or 1 oz. guava or apple jelly, a little balm and borage, sugar to taste, bottle soda-water; macerate the herb in the wine, strain clear; add the flavouring and the cider; sweeten to taste; pour in on a lump of ice in a covered vessel; add soda-water just before using.

No. 4.—Infuse in a gill of brandy, or whisky, 1 scruple of the essence of jargonelle pear (acetate of amyl), 2 dessert-spoonfuls of guava jelly, or quince; slice of cucumber, if desired, for a cool taste; quart of cider, bottle of perry, sugar to taste; add 3 bottles of lemonade or soda-water; ice up.

No. 5.—1 bottle of cider, ½ pint green ginger wine, 2 bottles ginger beer, tablespoonful pounded sugar; mix in a jug containing a 1 lb. lump of Lake ice.

Cider Nectar (*a la Harold Littledale*), No. 6.—1 quart cider, 1 bottle soda-water, ½ glass of sherry, 1 small glass of brandy, juice of J lemon (strained), ¼ of a lemon rubbed on sugar; sugar and nutmeg to taste; a sprig of verbena; flavour it to taste with extract of pine-apple; strain and ice well. This cup well deserves all the praise it has received.

No. 7.—Bottle of sparkling cider, ½ pint of dry sherry, liqueur-glass of Curaçoa, quart of shaven ice

Cider Cup (*for a Gathering*).—10 bottles of sparkling cider, 3 ditto sparkling perry, quart of rough cider, ½ pint of lemon-juice (strained), pint of orange-juice (strained), the oleo-saccharum of 3 oranges and 3 lemons, bottle of orange-brandy, 10 drops (or more to taste, if required) of essence of apple; mix well together; sweeten to taste, and add 1 quart of shaven ice and 8 bottles of potass water; keep iced till required; freeze up as much as possible.

Ale and Beer Cups should be made with good sound ale, and drunk from the tankard; being more palatable and presentable in this way than in glasses.

Cambridge Ale Cup.—Boil in 3 pints of water 1 oz. of cloves, 1 oz. of cinnamon, 1 oz. of mace, (all bruised together), for one hour; strain clear; add 3 oz. pounded sugar, with the juice and thin peel of a lemon; then 3 pints of good college ale, and ½ pint of sherry; make hot immediately before serving; add a thin slice of fresh toast, with some nutmeg grated on it.

Ale Cup.—Macerate ¼ oz. cinnamon, 2 cloves, 1 allspice, a little grated nutmeg, in a gill of sherry; in two hours, strain; press, and put this in a jug; pour in 2 pints Burton ale (No. 1), and 4 bottles Rawlings' ginger beer. This is a drink that will make you forget all care; a little ice is an improvement in the glass.

Ale Cup, or Jehu's Nectar.—Into a quart pot grate some ginger; add a wine-glass of gin-and-bitters; then a pint of good ale (heated). This should be drunk while it is frothing.

Ale Cup.—Bottle of Edinburgh ale, 2 bottles of ginger beer, ½ gill syrup from preserved ginger, slice of cucumber, pint of shaven ice; mix together; stir well, and pour into thin glasses.

Ale Cup.—Bottle of good ale; pint of lumps of ice.

Loving Cup.—1 pint of Mountain, 1 pint of Madeira, 1 pint of Lisbon, 1 bottle of champagne, 1 gill of Cognac, juice of 1 lemon, peel of half another rubbed on sugar; sweeten and spice to taste; when well mixed, strain clear; on serving, add ice.

Loving Cup.—Into a bowl put some toasts of bread; add 6 oz. of sugar (1 lump saturated with orange-flower water); grate ½ nutmeg; add equal quantities of cinnamon and ginger, in powder; pour on a quart of good ale, 1 bottle of sherry, and, immediately before drinking, 1 bottle of soda-water.

Councillor's Cup.—Rinds of 2 oranges, rubbed off with sugar, and steeped in ½ pint of brandy, which add to the strained juice of 1 lemon and ½ pint of orange-juice, and a pint of water; sweeten to taste, and mix. This can be used either as a cool or hot cup.

Porter Cup.—Bottle of porter, wine-glass of sherry, ½ bottle of claret, ½ nutmeg (grated), sugar to taste. Mix the nutmeg and sherry; in a quarter of an hour, strain; put these together, in a jug, with a slice of cucumber and a large lump of ice.

Porter Cup.—Bottle of Burton (No. 1), bottle of London porter, pint of shaven ice, bottle of lemonade.

Hot Cup.—Warm a pint of good ale; add 1 oz. of sugar, 1 oz. of mixed spice, glass of sherry; when nearly boiling, pour it on a round of buttered toast.

'Tween-Deck Cup, or a Splitting Headache.—Put into ¼ pint of rum ½ doz. crushed cloves, a little cinnamon, ginger, and nutmeg; strain in an hour, with pressure; add equal quantities of lime-juice, and 2 quarts of bottled ale.

Copus Cup.—Stick a lemon full of cloves, which roast before a fire till of a dark brown; while roasting, make a mixture of ¼ pint of brandy, ¼ pint of noyeau, ½ oz. cinnamon (bruised); let this be well stirred; then put the lemon into a bowl, give it a squeeze with a spoon; add a toast of bread, and lay the lemon on the bread; add 4 oz. pounded sugar; pour on 2 quarts of hot old ale; then add the spirits, and in a quarter of an hour it will be fit for use.

Ale Cup.—Bottle of Scotch ale, mixed spice and nutmeg on a toast of bread; pour through a strainer, on a lump of ice; drink immediately.

Ale Cup.—Grate ¼ oz. nutmeg; add an equal quantity of pounded ginger, cinnamon, and 3 oz. brown sugar; beat these up with the yolks of 3 eggs; meanwhile warm ½ gallon good ale and ½ pint of gin; pour in, whisking the while the spice mixture, when all frothing: it must be drunk immediately.

Freemasons' Cup.—Pint of Scotch ale, pint of mild beer, ½ pint of brandy, 1 pint of sherry, ½ lb. crushed sugar-candy; grated nutmeg to taste. This can be used either as a hot or cold cup.

Wait a Bit.—Pint bottle of the best Scotch ale; 1 bottle of aërated lemonade, pint of ice in lumps.

Mother-in-law.—Half old and half bitter ale.

Shandy Gaff.—Pint of good ale, bottle of ginger beer.

Cooper.—pint of Dublin stout, pint of London porter.

John Bright.—Pint of stout, pint of bitter ale.

Purl, or Early Birds.—Heat a quart of ale, mixed with a tablespoonful of powdered ginger and nutmeg; whisk up with a gill of cold ale and 2 oz. moist sugar, 3 fresh eggs; when well frothed up, add the warm ale, by degrees, and a glass of spirits; when this is done, drink immediately.

Bishop à la Cutler.—Beat the yolks of 8 eggs well up in a basin; add 4 pints of whisky, and 2 pints of boiling milk; first add the milk to the eggs, then the whisky; sweeten to taste; grate in a little nutmeg and cloves.

A Good Bishop.—Stick a good lemon full of cloves, which roast before the fire till it becomes a rich dark brown; meanwhile pound together ½ lb. loaf-sugar, a little grated nutmeg, ginger, cinnamon, 2 cloves, 1 allspice, the thin rind of a lemon; place this mixture, when well incorporated, in a bowl by the side of the fire, adding ½ pint of water, ½ pint of port wine (or Roussillon), 1 bottle of claret; strain all through muslin; heat the mixture, but do not let it burn, and into the empty warm bowl drop in the lemon; give it a press with the spoon; add a wine-glass of cherry-brandy, and the mixture; keep it hot, and you will find this a really good bishop.

N.B.—This bishop can be made the day previous, and mulled when required for use; also used for port-wine cup.

Pope.—Roast 3 bitter Seville oranges to a pale brown colour, which lay in a heated vessel; add 1 lb. of pounded loaf-sugar, press the oranges and sugar together; add 2 bottles of mulled Burgundy, and 1 pint of hot water.

Cardinal.—Cut 3 Tangerine oranges in slices, add ¼ oz. bruised cinnamon (or 3 drops essence of cinnamon), a little mace, 3 drops essence of nutmeg, 3 bruised cardamom seeds, and 4 oz. of dissolved barley-sugar in 1 pint of hot water; cover, and let the mixture simmer for half an hour; strain clear with pressure; add 1 quart of Rhenish wine, which warm up; if too highly flavoured, add more wine.

N.B.—Cardinal is also made with champagne, and roasted orange infused in it.

Archbishop.—Stick a Seville orange full of cloves; roast it before a fire; cut it in halves, and cover it with sugar; add 1 bottle of mulled white wine, either sherry or Marsala.

N.B.—Claret is sometimes used for archbishop.

Beadle.—Pound ¼ oz. cinnamon, 4 cloves, and ½ oz. ginger together; add ¼ lb. of sugar and 1 pint of boiling water and strain; add the liquor carefully to 2 yolks of eggs; beat up, then 1 glass of raisin, and 6 glasses of ginger wine. To be drunk while in a state of froth.

Churchwarden.—Pour on a roasted lemon 1 bottle of mulled Roussillon; add 1 pint weak tea, sweetened with ¼ lb. sugar.

Chorister.—Beat up the yolks of 3 eggs with 3 tablespoonfuls of cold water; add when beaten up, stirring the while, a mixture made with ¼ pint of white wine, 2 drops of balsam of Peru, 2 oz. of sugar, and ¼ pint of water, all made hot. To be drunk while in a state of froth.

COCKTAILS are compounds very much used by "early birds" to fortify the inner man, and by those who like their consolations hot and strong. "Cocktail" is not so ancient an institution as Juleps, &c, but, with its next of kin, "Crusta," promises to maintain its ground.

Brandy or Gin Cocktail.—¼ pint of brandy or gin, ½ gill of Curaçoa, 1 tablespoonful of bitters, ½ gill of ginger syrup, 1 pint of ice; mix with a spoon; moisten the rim of the tumbler with juice of lemon.

Brandy Do.—¼ pint of brandy, 2 fluid drachms of essence of ginger; sweeten to taste, and fill up with hot water.

Whisky Do.—Piece of lemon-peel, 2 fluid drachms of tincture of calumba, 2 drops tincture of capsicum, ½ gill of whisky; infuse these, and strain; add 1 pint of ice; or drink warm, if preferred.

Whisky Cocktail.—½ gill of whisky, 1 teaspoonful of bitters, 2 drops essence of cinnamon; sweeten with syrup; add ½ lb. of ice, pounded.

Cider Cocktail.—1 pint of good cider, sweetened to taste, slice of lemon, ½ pint of shaven ice, or iced aërated water, 1 drop of tincture of calumba: further improved by a tablespoonful of Curaçoa.

Crusta of Brandy, Whisky, or Gin.—Peel a lemon to the core, in one large curl; put this in a goblet; add pounded sugar, brandy, and ice, or other spirit.

Juleps.—Of this class of drinks, that nectarous compound "Mint Julep" is the most popular in this country. It is an especial favourite with the Americans, especially down South. It was first brought into vogue here by Captain Marryat, who, in his work on America, says:—"I must descant a little upon the mint julep, as it is, with the thermometer at 100°, one of the most delightful and insinuating potations that ever was invented, and may be drunk with equal satisfaction when the thermometer is as low as 70°. There are many varieties, such as those composed of Claret, Madeira, &c, but the ingredients of the real mint julep are as follows. I learned how to make them, and succeeded pretty well. Put into a tumbler about a dozen of the tender shoots of mint; upon them put a spoonful of white sugar, and equal proportions of peach and common brandy, so as to fill up one-third, or perhaps a little less. Then take rasped or pounded ice, and fill up the tumbler. Epicures rub the lips of the tumbler with a piece of fresh pine-apple, and the tumbler itself is often incrusted outside with stalactites of ice. As the ice melts, you drink."

Another Mint Julep.—"Take 3 sprigs of fresh-gathered mint; put them into a soda-water glass; add 2 tablespoonfuls of sugar, glass of brandy, juice of 1 orange; in ten minutes, fill the glass up with shaven ice; draw the mint out, and re-arrange them, stem upwards; lay the thin peel of orange on top; pour on 1 tablespoonful of rum and 1 tablespoonful of white sugar-candy, crushed; suck through straws—let me add—devoutly."

Pine-apple Julep.—1 pint of pine-apple ice, or a fresh one sliced; juice of 3 oranges; 1 gill of gin; 1 bottle of Moselle; 1 pint of pounded ice.

Whisky Julep.—Put a few tops of mint into a tumbler; add 2 tablespoonfuls of sugar and 3 of water; ¼ pint of whisky; thin peel of a quarter of a lemon; in five minutes fill up with shaven ice; in drinking use straws, or a stick of maccaroni.

Gin Julep.—4 sprigs of mint, 1 gill of gin, ½ gill of Maraschino, 1 pint of pounded ice; use straws.

White-wine Julep.—Two or three sprigs of mint, ½ oz. of sugar, ¼ pint of any kind of white wine; fill up with shaven ice; lay a slice of lemon on top, with pounded barley-sugar; use straws.

Season Ticket.—Put into an ice pitcher 1 bottle of cider, 1 gill of good lemonade, 2 glasses of dry sherry, 1 teaspoonful of orange-flower water, 3 sprigs of mint; sweeten to taste; add 1 lb. of shaven ice.

Mulled Egg-wine.—Beat up an egg with 3 glasses of sherry and teaspoonful of sugar; add some grated ginger, and carefully ½ pint boiling water, stirring the while; grate on a little nutmeg before serving.

Sleeper.—Boil in ½ pint of water 6 cloves, ¼ oz. cinnamon (bruised), 8 coriander seeds, 1 ½ oz. sugar; strain, and add juice of ½ lemon, and ¼ pint of old rum; break the yolks of two eggs in a basin; pour in the mixture gradually, whisking the while; when well frothed, strain through a sieve into a large tumbler.

Locomotive.—Make 1 pint of red Roussillon or Burgundy nearly boil; beat up 2 yolks of eggs with 1 oz. of honey, 1 drop of essence of cinnamon, 3 drops essence of cloves, and ¼ gill of Curaçoa; when well frothed, add the hot wine; drink hot, and it will drive away care.

Hot Egg-nogg, or "Auld Man's Milk.".—Heat a pint of Scotch ale; add while warming ¼ oz. bruised cinnamon, ¼ oz. grated nutmeg, ¼ oz. powdered ginger; beat up the yolks of 2 eggs with a little brown sugar; pour in the ale gradually; when well amalgamated, add glass of whisky.

Baltimore Egg-nogg.—Beat up the yolks of 3 eggs, and ¼ of a nutmeg grated, with 2 oz. of pounded sugar, to the consistence of cream; add, pouring in quietly the while, ½ gill of brandy or rum, and glass of Marsala or brown sherry; add the whites of the eggs (well beaten to a good froth), and, when well incorporated, gill of cream and pint of milk. This is not a warm drink, and is easily digestible; it forms a nourishing dietetic beverage for debilitated persons.

Iced Egg-nogg.—Beat up the yolk of 1 egg with a tablespoonful of cold water and same of pounded white sugar; add 1 gill of sherry or ½ gill brandy, ditto of rum, ¼ pint good milk; mix together; add ¼ pint shaven (or pulverized) ice.

General Harrison's Egg-nogg.—1 egg, 1 teaspoonful of sugar, 3 lumps of ice in a tumbler; fill the tumbler with cider; well shake up.

Excellent Negus.—1 bottle of sherry (or port), 2 ½ pints of water, juice of 1 lemon, a little of the peel rubbed off on sugar; grated nutmeg, and sugar to taste; add 1 drop essence of ambergris, or 10 drops essence of vanilla; all to be made and drunk warm.

Gin or Whisky Sling.—To 1 gill gin or whisky add tablespoonful of powdered sugar in a soda-water glass, filled with shaven ice; use straws.

Toddy.—Use equal quantities of spirits and hot water, add sugar to taste.

Apple Toddy.—Put a baked apple in a glass; add 1 oz. of powdered sugar, 1 gill of brandy, ½ pint boiling cider; grate a little ginger on top of liquor; piece of lemon-peel.

Whisky Sling.—Thin peel of an orange or lemon soaked in ¼ pint of gin or whisky; juice of 2 oranges and 1 lemon; sugar to taste; add 1 pint of pounded Lake ice; use straws.

Claret Granato.—2 bottles claret, ½ bottle sherry, pint of clear orangeade, ¼ pint syrup of capillaire; mix well together; immerse in freezer; half freeze and serve.

Brandy Smash.—2 sprigs of mint, wine-glass of brandy; sugar to taste; fill up with pounded ice; lay 2 slices of orange on top; use straws.

No. 2.—2 slices of lemon, 2 slices of pine-apple, 1 glass of brandy, 2 tablespoonfuls of sugar; fill with pounded Lake ice; use straws.

Hollands, Gin, or Whisky Smash.—3 sprigs of mint, 1 of verbena, 1 gill of Hollands; tablespoonful of white sugar; fill up with shaven Lake ice; use straws.

Cobbler is very similar to mint julep and smash: it is an American invention, but has become an universal favourite, and is generally made with wine, instead of spirit.

Sherry Ditto.—¼ pint of sherry, 1 oz. of sugar, 3 slices of orange, or a few strawberries or raspberries; if liked, a

little powdered cinnamon or grated nutmeg on top; fill
up the tumbler with planed ice; use straws.

Ditto.—½ pint of sherry, ½ gill of Curaçoa, thin peel of 1
orange, juice of the same, pint of pounded ice; tablespoonful of sugar on top; use straws.

Champagne Ditto.—Pieces of orange and lemon peel, ½ gill
citronelle, put in a glass half full of ice; fill up with champagne; use straws.

Hock Ditto.—Piece of orange-peel, and the juice of one;
sugar; fill up with hock and shaven ice; use straws.

Claret Cobbler.—The same, using claret.

Sauterne Ditto.—The same, using Sauterne.

Port or Sherry Cobbler, or Sangaree.—½ pint brown sherry,
2 tablespoonfuls of powdered sugar; slice of pine-apple;
pounded ice; grate some nutmeg on top; use straws.

Brandy Sangaree.—1 gill of brandy; 1 gill of water, a teaspoonful of sugar in a large glass; fill nearly to the brim
with ice, and pour on the top a glass of port wine.

Nectar.—Raisins (chopped), 2 lbs.; honey, 4 lbs.; juice of 2
lemons strained, the peel of same, rubbed off on sugar,
2 gallons of water (boiling); when cool, add 3 bottles of
sherry, or 3 pints of rum, or brandy, or gin, mixed; strain
with expression in 14 days; filter clear; bottle.

Soda Nectar.—Juice of 1 lemon, strained; three-quarters of
a tumblerful of water; sugar to taste; ½ teaspoonful carbonate of soda; mix, and drink while effervescing,

Nectar—for 90° in the Shade.—Put a lemon ice in a soda-
water glass; add ½ gill of whisky and a bottle of iced
soda-water.

Spider.—Gill of gin, bottle of lemonade, ½ pint lumps of ice.

Stone Fence.—Gill of whisky, ½ pint of cider, ½ pint of shaven ice.

Stone Wall.—Equal quantities of brandy and shaven ice; add bottle of iced soda-water.

Saloop.—Make a decoction of 1 oz. of salep; strain; add 1 pint boiling water.

Rumfustian.—Put ½ bottle sherry in a saucepan; add ¼ oz. bruised cinnamon, ¼ grated nutmeg, 3 bruised cardamom seeds, 2 oz. sugar, thin rind of lemon; well digest by side of fire till nearly boiling, during which whisk up yolks of 3 eggs, with 1 pint of ale and ½ pint of gin; when ready, pour the sherry in through a strainer, stirring the while.

Prima Donna.—Beat yolk of 1 egg in a glass of sherry; add a very little cayenne pepper.

Hour Before.—Wine-glass of dry sherry or Madeira, with a dash of Boker's or Angostura bitters.

Ribs.—Gill of Cognac brandy; gill of shaven ice; tablespoonful Arabic gum syrup.

Ice-Cream Soda-Water.—Equal quantity of fruit syrup and cream; double the same of shaven ice; add bottle of soda-water, and drink off.

Ching Ching.—Gill of old rum, 1 sliced orange, 1 drop of essence of peppermint, 2 drops essence of cloves on sugar; mix in soda-water tumbler; fill up with pounded ice.

Tickle my Fancy.—Boil together 1 gill of lemon-juice, 1 pint of calves-foot jelly, 1 lb. of stoned raisins, ½ lb. of sugar, 1 pint of water; when cool, add 1 gallon of cider; strain with pressure; add to this liquid a liqueur made by macerating, in a quart of brandy and pint of raisin wine (or sherry),

cloves, cinnamon, ground ginger, lemon-peel, equal
weights, as per strength desired; strain with pressure;
filter clear.

Apple-Water.—Boil 12 pippins and 1 quince in 2 quarts of
water; strain with pressure; add honey or sugar.

Apple-Water.—Bake 12 apples and 1 pear; when well baked,
put them into a pitcher; add thin peel of a lemon, 1 oz.
grated ginger; pour on boiling water; strain with pressure
when cool.

Aleberry.—Mix 3 spoonfuls of fine oatmeal with quart of old
ale; boil, strain clear, and sweeten; add juice of 1 lemon,
½ grated nutmeg, some powdered ginger, ½ pint of grape
wine; put a toast of bread on the surface of the liquor.

Ale Posset.—To a quart of ale add a round of buttered toast;
let it soak in the ale; grate nutmeg on the bread, also
sugar; and 1 pint of sherry; serve hot.

"Arf-and-Arf."—The London mixture is, ½ pint porter, and
½ pint ale; the New York, ½ pint old ale, and ½ pint of
new.

Asses' Milk.—½ gill of rum; bottle of aërated lemonade.

Ale Posset, "Sir Walter Raleigh's."—Take ½ pint of white wine
(a dry sherry is best), ½ pint good clear ale; add quart
of boiled cream, flavoured with spices; strain through a
tammy. This and treacle posset is a favourite remedy for
colds, being a hot "night-cap."

Birthday Syllabub.—Juice of 2 lemons, ½ lb. of sugar, mixed in
a bowl; add pint of sherry; grate in a nutmeg; add 2 quarts
new milk; in serving, let the curd remain in the glass.

Black Currant Drink.—½ pint of juice, 1 quart weak green
tea; sugar to taste.

Black Stripe.—To a wine-glass of rum add 1 drop of pine-apple oil, and ½ oz. of molasses. This drink can be used with hot water, or snow ice.

Brandy Champerelle.—Wine-glass of Curaçoa, wine-glass of brandy, wine-glass of bitters; mix with ice.

Egg Flip.—Into a clean saucepan put 1 quart of good ale; then beat up in a basin the yolks of 6 fresh eggs; into which grate half a nutmeg and ½ lb. of moist sugar, wine-glass of gin or whisky; beat up thoroughly well together; as the ale simmers, skim the froth off into a basin containing the mixture; when the ale nearly boils (do not let it boil) pour it into the mixture, stirring the while. If you use the whites of eggs as well, only use 3 eggs.

Lamb's Wool.—Roast 8 apples; mash them, and add 1 quart of old ale; press and strain; add ginger and nutmeg (grated); sweeten to taste; warm, and drink while warm.

Wassail Bowl.—To 1 quart of hot ale add grated nutmeg, ginger, and cinnamon, of each ¼ oz., and ½ bottle of sherry, 2 good slices of toasted bread, juice of 1 lemon, peel of same, and 2 well-roasted apples; sweeten to taste.

Mulled Wine.—Into a stewpan put 3 bruised cloves, ½ stick of cinnamon, ½ peel of a lemon, 4 oz. loaf-sugar, ½ pint of water; boil for a quarter of an hour; then add a little grated nutmeg, pint of claret, wine-glass of port wine; when nearly boiled, strain, either on toasted bread or otherwise.

Wine Whey.—Boil 1 pint of milk; when boiled, add 2 glasses of sherry, rhubarb, or currant wine; when it again boils, draw from the fire; strain from curd, and sweeten to taste.

Floster.—A gill of sherry, ½ gill noyeau, 1 oz. sugar, bottle of iced lemonade, ½ pint of ice.

Toast-and-water.—Toast a crust of bread gradually to a chocolate brown; add the toast to a jug of boiling water; when
cold, strain; it is much preferable to put the toast to the
water.

West Country Syllabub.—Put in a bowl 1 pint of port wine, 1
pint of sherry; sweeten to taste; add 2 quarts of new milk;
in half an hour cover well with clotted cream, with some
grated nutmeg and cinnamon.

Negus.—Peel a lemon very thin; add juice of same and bottle
of wine; sugar to taste, and boiling water according to
strength desired.

Sir Walter Scott's Wassail Bowl.—Place 1 lb. of sponge cake,
1 lb. of ratafias and macaroons in a bowl; add wine-glass
of sherry, 2 bottles of raisin wine, bottle of champagne,
bottle of Chablis, and a little lemon-juice if desired.

Pope's Posset.—Bruise 1 lb. of Jordan almonds, which boil
in a pint of boiling water for 20 minutes; add a bottle of
Marsala and wine-glass of brandy, and 2 oz. white sugar;
strain; add pint of boiling water to the residue, which
again strain and mix with the liquor; serve hot.

Eau Sucré.—½ lb. sugar to 1 pint of boiling water.

Excellent Egg-flip.—1 gill of good French brandy, yolks of 2
eggs, 1 gill of cinnamon-water, 2 drops oil of cinnamon.
This agreeable stimulant and restorative is of great service when used in cases of extreme exhaustion.

Brandy Punch—A Sensation.—Tablespoonful of raspberry
syrup, mixed with a gill of water; add 2 tablespoonfuls of
white sugar, 1 ½ brandy, juice of ½ lemon and ½ orange,
1 slice of pine-apple; fill the tumbler with shaven ice;
and smile.

Lait de Poule.—Mix the yolks of 2 eggs with 2 oz. powdered sugar; add tablespoonful orange-flower water; beat up well, and add ½ pint boiling water.

Hippocras, Red.—1 oz. cinnamon, 1 drachm coriander seeds, blade of mace, ½ grated nutmeg, 1 oz. bruised ginger, 3 musk mallow seeds, beaten to a powder together; add juice of ½ lemon, gill of brandy; strain clear; 2 pints of syrup, 1 bottle of claret, and pint of boiling water.

Lait Sucré.—1 lemon (sliced), ¼ lb. loaf-sugar, boiled in a pint of milk.

White-wine Whey.—Into ½ pint boiling milk put 2 oz. loaf-sugar, and 2 wine-glasses of white wine; a light floating curd will be perceived; boil for a few minutes; strain, and serve hot. The curd should not be eaten, being indigestible.

Hot Spiced Ale.—Boil 1 quart of good ale; add ½ grated nutmeg; beat up 2 eggs; mix them with a little cold ale; when ready, add the warm ale; keep stirring to a froth; add a piece of butter; serve with dry toast.

Parisian Pousse Cafe.—Teaspoonful of Kirschwasser, 1 fluid drachm teaspoonful of Curaçoa, ditto ½ teaspoonful of Chartreuse.

Pousse l'Amour.—Put the yolk of an egg into a wine-glass; half cover it with Maraschino; add a little vanilla cordial, and some brandy; and smile.

Negus.—Quart of boiling water, pint of port (or Roussillon) wine, ½ lb. loaf-sugar, juice and zest of a lemon, juice of 2 oranges, little powdered cinnamon and nutmeg to taste; mix when cool; strain, and serve warm; sherry or any other wine can be substituted for the port, but port-wine negus is usually made.

Soda Negus.—Put ½ pint port wine into a saucepan, with 4 lumps of sugar, 3 cloves, and enough grated nutmeg to cover a shilling; warm; do not suffer it to boil; pour into a jug; on the warm wine pour a bottle of soda-water.

Mulled Wine.—In mulling wine, care must be taken that the vessel is perfectly clean; otherwise, if it is greasy, or impregnated with any other flavour, it is apt to impart it, and spoil the wine; boil the spices for a short time; add the sugar, when it is well dissolved, to the wine, which on no account let boil. In mulling wine with eggs, pour the boiling liquor on the eggs, stirring the while; if you pour the eggs into the liquor, the yolks will curdle.

To Mull Wine.—Into a clean stewpan pour 1 pint of water; add ½ oz. of bruised ginger, cinnamon, cloves, nutmeg, the spices most likely to predominate; cover up, and boil down to ½ pint of water; then strain clear, and add ¼ lb. of sugar and 1 pint of claret.

Ditto, à la Coleman.—Into 1 ½ pint of water boil 1 Tangerine orange, and ¼ oz. of cinnamon to a pint; strain with pressure; sweeten with ½ lb. of sugar; add pint of raisin or green ginger wine.

Mulled Wine, with Eggs,—

> "First, my dear madam, you must take
> Nine eggs, which carefully you'll break;
> Into a bowl you'll drop the white,
> The yolks into another by it.
> Let Betsy beat the whites with a switch,
> Till they appear quite froth'd and rich.
> Another hand the yolks must beat

With sugar, which will make them sweet;
Three or four spoonfuls maybe'll do,
Though some, perhaps, would take but two.
Into a skillet next you'll pour
A bottle of good wine, or more;
Put half a pint of water, too,
Or it may prove too strong for you:
And while the eggs by two are beating,
The wine and water may be heating;
But, when it comes to boiling heat,
The yolks and whites together beat.
With half a pint of water more—
Mixing them well—then gently pour
Into the skillet with the wine,
And stir it briskly all the time.
Then pour it off into a pitcher;
Grate nutmeg in to make it richer;
Then drink it hot, for he's a fool
Who lets such precious liquor cool."

Red or White Currant Water.—1 quart of red or white currant juice, clear; add 1 gill of raspberry vinegar or syrup; sweeten to taste; ½ gallon water; ½ gill brandy.

Black Currant.—Pint of juice, ¼ pint green tea, ½ gill spirits; sugar; water to taste.

Cherry.—Pound 2 lbs. Kentish cherries into a mass, stones and kernels; add juice of 1 lemon; pint of boiling water; sugar to taste.

Spring Fruit.—Boil 10 sticks of rhubarb; strain; sweeten to taste.

Raspberry and Strawberry.—Pint of juice, gill of either syrup.

Effervescing.—Put fruit into good vinegar (diluted acetic acid best), adding fresh fruit till sufficiently strong; when required for use, dissolve a little carbonate of soda in a small quantity of water, and dash it in.

Orangeade.—Mix a pint of clear orange-juice, pint of syrup, ½ pint of lemon-juice, 2 drops of neroli; dilute with water as desired.

Knickerbocker à la Monsieur.—To the strained juice of 1 lemon, or orange, add 2 tablespoonfuls of raspberry syrup, 1 wine-glass of Jamaica rum, tablespoonful of Curaçoa; mix in soda-water glass; add balance with shaven ice.

Knickerbocker à la Madame.—½ pint lemon-water ice, ½ pint sherry or Madeira, 1 bottle seltzer water, ¼ pint shaven ice.

White Lion.—Rind of lime or lemon in soda-water glass; pour in equal quantities of raspberry syrup, rum, and Curaçoa; sweeten to taste; add shaven ice to top of glass; rub the rim of glass with a slice of pine-apple.

St. Charles.—Cherry-water ice, 1 pint; gill of Kirschwasser; ½ pint shaven ice; bottle seltzer water.

Benson Hill.—Fill tumbler two-thirds with lemonade, wine-glass of brandy; fill up with green lime-shrub.

PUNCH

"Whene'er a bowl of punch we make,
Four striking opposites we take—
The strong, the small, the sharp, the sweet,
Together mixed, most kindly meet.
And when they happily unite,
The bowl is 'fragrant with delight.'"

This delicious beverage, which, if compounded in a proper manner, is not so intoxicating as it has the character of being, is a composition of sugar, lemon, water, or milk, and spirit, with the addition of some aromatic or cordial; wine being sometimes substituted for the spirit. There is no precise rule for making punch, no two persons agreeing in the exact proportions of the ingredients. The great secret is that the mixture should be so happily compounded that nothing predominates. For making punch—in fact, in everything in which lemons are used—the peel should be cut very thin, by reason that the flavour and scent, which constitute its most valuable properties, reside in minute cells, close to the surface of the fruit, so, by slicing it very thin, the whole of the minute receptacles are cut through, and double the quantity of the oil is obtained; or the outer rind may be rubbed with a lump of sugar, which, as it breaks the delicate vessels, absorbs the ambrosial essence. To make the sugared essence (or oleo-saccharum), either pursue the above method, and as the sugar is impregnated with the essence, scrape it off with a knife from the lump, or peel some lemons very thin, and pound the peel into a stiff dry paste in a marble mortar, with sufficient sugar, and preserve it for use, closely pressed in a tightly covered jar.

Orange and lemon juice are best strained clear from pip or pulp; it can be brought quite clear by filtering it through washed sand. To preserve the juice for a time, a little spirit must be added. To economize juice, diluted citric acid is generally used. A decoction of tea, especially a mixture of green and Pekoe, is preferred to water for the liquor of punch.

In making hot punch, put the spirits in before the liquor, which is better "off the boil."

Punch is much improved by adding a very small quantity (which the size of the bowl will regulate) of flowers of benzoin; it imparts the flavour of arrack to the punch.

A piece of butter, about the size of a filbert nut, is used by many people to soften punch; this size will be sufficient for a quart.

Guava or apple jelly makes punch truly delicious.

The following formula will give a good idea of the general method of preparing punch on a rather large scale:—

Begin by paring the rinds of 30 lemons very thin; pound them in a mortar with sufficient sugar to form a dry stiff paste; strain the juice; collect the pips, which put in a saucepan, and pour on them a pint of boiling water; keep hot, so as to draw out the thick mucilaginous flavour; mix together and strain clear, adding a little boiling water to the remains in the strainer; when ready, taste the sherbet; add more acid, or sugar, if required, and the liquor (tea or water); to every quart of sherbet add ½ pint of rum, and 1 pint of brandy. This punch, if not made too weak with liquor, will keep some time. It can also have whatever addition the taste or fancy of the manipulator may choose to prescribe for the sake of variety.[*]

Tolpsey's Account of a West India Planter's Punch.—"He made his appearance with a respectably sized bowl, an enormous jug of boiling water, and a large paper bag filled with sugar. Our punch-maker then commenced operations, and having extracted from his secret store a bottle of his matchless rum, his limes, and a small pot of guava jelly, he brewed about a pint of green tea (2 oz.), and, the infusion finished, two-thirds of the sugar was dissolved in it. After the tea leaves had been thrown

---

[*] Although the proportions may in many of the recipes be given in large quantities, they can easily be reduced by taking half, or a quarter, or even less, of each ingredient named.

aside, the remainder of the sugar was rubbed on the lime;
Mr. Hamilton observing that the essential oil, which
conveyed the exquisite flavour, was much more strongly
diffused throughout the compound than when the skin
was peeled; then the delicious acid of the fruit was added
to the already impregnated sugar, and as soon as the
several lumps had imbibed the proportions required, the
guava jelly (and without this confection no punch can be
pronounced perfect) was dissolved in a pint or so of boiling water. This done, the tea, the sweets, and the acids
were commingled, and the foundation or sherbet tasted
by the experienced palate of the grand compounder; six
glasses of Cognac, two of Madeira, and the bottle of old
rum were added, and over all about a quart more of boiling water, and, as a finishing touch, the slightest possible
sprinkling of nutmeg."

Punch à la Regent, by P. Watier, Royal Lodge, 1820: *original.—*
Take 4 oz. of clarified sugar, thin peel of 1 lemon and 1
Seville orange, 1 bottle of dry champagne, ½ bottle of
white brandy, ½ gill of rum, ½ gill of arrack, ½ gill of pine-
apple syrup, 1 wine-glass of Maraschino; pour 1 quart of
boiling water over 2 teaspoonfuls of green tea; let it stand
five minutes; strain, and mix with other ingredients; pass
through a sieve; let it remain in ice 30 minutes.

*Cutler's Rum Punch.—*1 bottle of brandy, 1 pint of rum, ½
pint of sherry, juice of 3 lemons, a little grated nutmeg,
lemon-peel, 1 quart of boiling water; put the thin paring
of 2 lemons into a mortar with ½ lb. of sugar; beat into
a mass; strain the lemon-juice, which add; mix well, and
put the ingredients into a jug; then add the sherry, rum,

brandy, and, lastly, the boiling water; in a quarter of an hour it will be ready to drink.

Coleman's Rum Punch (E. G. Coleman).—1 pint of rum, 1 pint of shrub, 1 ½ pint of pale brandy, liqueur-glass of Maraschino or Curaçoa, ¼ lb. of loaf-sugar, teaspoonful of citric acid, half a gallon of boiling water.

Oxford Punch.—Put the thinly-pared peelings of 4 lemons and 2 Seville oranges into a mortar containing ½ lb. loaf-sugar, which beat up into a smooth mass; into which squeeze the juice of the fruit, adding juice of 4 sweet oranges, and ½ pint of water; strain the mixture into a jug (standing close to the fire); add 1 pint of calves-foot jelly, which thoroughly incorporate; pour in 2 quarts of boiling water, ½ pint of syrup, teaspoonful of orange-flower water, wine-glass of Curaçoa, ½ pint of sherry, pint of Cognac brandy, pint of pine-apple rum, quart of orange-shrub; stir well together.

Bannister's Milk Punch, 1829.—Pare 18 lemons very thin; steep the same three days in 1 quart best old rum; then add 2 quarts best brandy, the juice of 9 Seville oranges and 9 lemons, 3 quarts of water, 3 lbs. of double-refined sugar, and 2 grated nutmegs; when the sugar is dissolved, mix thoroughly; add 2 quarts scalded milk; cover, and let stand two hours; then clear it through a tammy, and bottle; when required for use, it should be iced 20 minutes before drinking.

Cambridge Milk Punch.—Boil in 2 quarts of new milk 1 dozen bruised bitter almonds, and paring of 2 lemons, and ½ lb. loaf-sugar; when well flavoured, strain clear and keep warm; stir in the well-whisked whites of 3 eggs, which have been mixed with a little cold milk; while still

stirring, add ½ pint of rum and 1 pint of brandy; mull the
punch to a froth, and serve immediately in glasses.

Milk Punch for Immediate Use.—½ pint strained lemon-juice,
3 drops essence of lemon, 1 gill of ginger syrup, 1 gill of
real (or mock) arrack; 1 ½ pint of brandy, ½ pint of rum,
1 lb. of loaf-sugar; dissolve the essence in the spirits; mix
together; add ½ pint boiling water; in a quarter of an hour
add 3 pints of boiled milk; strain through a tammy; add
½ oz. of isinglass; when clarified, serve.

G. M. Gurton's Punch.—½ pint of rum, ½ pint of sherry, ½
pint of brown brandy, 1 gill of Curaçoa, 1 pint of lime-
juice, 1 gill of ginger syrup; mix together, and add to 3
pints of an infusion of weak green tea; sweeten to taste;
mix well. This can be used either as a hot or iced drink;
if iced, use more liquor, from 4 to 5 pints.

Tea Punch.—Make an infusion of 1 ½ oz. mixed green and
orange Pekoe tea, with a quart of boiling water; strain
clear as possible; place a bright metal bowl before the
fire, so that it will become quite hot; well mix 1 drachm of
citric acid, 1 drop essence of neroli, 1 lb. loaf-sugar, 1 pint
of brandy, 1 pint of rum; thoroughly mix; put the mixture
in the hot bowl, and set fire to it; while burning, gradually
pour in the tea; keep stirring, and serve while blazing.

Yankee Punch.—drop on each of 2 lumps of sugar 4 drops
essence of vanilla, 2 drops essence of ambergris, which
put into a bottle containing 1 pint of brandy; when well
digested, add to it 1 pint of lemon-juice, 1 pint of lemon
syrup, ½ bottle of port wine, 1 bottle Roussillon or Claret,
dessert-spoonful of orange-flower water; sweeten according to taste, and add as much water as required.

Francatelli's Rum Punch.—Into a vessel holding 2 gallons put
1 quart of brandy, 1 quart of rum, ½ pint of old arrack, ½
pint strong-made green tea, juice of 12 lemons, thin rind
of 4 lemons, a nutmeg grated, stick of cinnamon (well
bruised), 12 cloves (bruised), 30 coriander seeds (bruised),
2 lbs. pine-apple (sliced), 9 lbs. lump-sugar, 2 quarts boiling water; stir together; tie a bladder over top of pitcher;
let it steep undisturbed for two days; boil 2 quarts pure
milk; add this to the other ingredients; mix thoroughly;
in an hour afterwards filter the punch through a clean
tammy bag; when filtered, bottle off the punch, and cork
down tight; keep the bottles in a good cellar. This is a
truly excellent punch, but it should be iced for use.

Billy Dawson's Punch.—Steep the thin paring of 1 lemon
in 1 gill of rum, 1 gill of brandy, ½ gill of arrack, ½ gill
of brown stout; strain, and sweeten to taste; add 1 pint
boiling water, with a little lemon-juice.

Trinidad Punch.—In 1 pint of rum digest 1 oz. chocolate, ½
stick vanilla; when well incorporated, strain; add 2 pints
cocoa-nut milk. This punch can be used either as a cool
cup, with ice, or hot.

Mississippi Punch.—Wine-glass of peach brandy, wine-glass
of arrack, peel and juice of 1 lemon, wine-glass of rum;
sugar to taste; quart of shaven ice.

Vauxhall Souvenir Punch.—Pint of sherry, ½ pint of mock
arrack, a little essence of lemon, rubbed on sugar; add
as much water, or weak tea, as desired; sweeten to taste.

Roderick Random, or Bumbo Punch.—Grate a nutmeg into
1 pint of rum; let it digest two days; strain; add pint of
water; sufficient sugar to taste.

Brandy Punch.—An American Sensation.—Tablespoonful raspberry syrup, mixed with 1 gill of water, and 2 table-spoonfuls of white sugar; juice of ½ lemon and 1 orange, strained; add slice of pine-apple and 1 gill of brandy; fill the tumbler with shaven ice.

Ruby Punch.—Dissolve in 3 pints of weak green-tea 1 lb. of sugar; add strained juice of 6 lemons, 1 pint of arrack, and 1 pint of port wine; sweeten to taste.

Russian Punch.—Same as Ruby; but use gill of Kümmel instead of the arrack and wine.

Vanilla.—Infuse a stick of vanilla in ½ pint of pale brandy; when sufficiently flavoured, strain; add a sherbet of lemon-juice and sugar; fill the tumbler with shaven ice, and use straws.

Royal Punch.—1 ½ pint of green tea, ½ pint of brandy, ¼ pint of pine-apple rum, ditto Curaçoa, ditto arrack, juice of 2 lemons (strained), the peel of 1 rubbed off on sugar; warm, and add 1 gill of hot calves-foot jelly; serve hot.

Regent's Punch.—Bottle of sparkling champagne, bottle of hock, gill of dry sherry, gill of pale brandy, ½ gill of rum, gill of lemon-juice, ½ gill of Curaçoa, quart of green tea, bottle of seltzer water; sugar to taste; ice to the utmost.

Guy's Punch.—Rub the outside of 3 citrons and 3 lemons with a lump of sugar till all the essential oil is absorbed; in a stewpan put 6 cloves, 1 stick of vanilla, 2 sticks of cinnamon (well bruised together); add 1 lb. of sugar and 1 ½ pint of hot water; simmer for six hours; strain with pressure; add the clear juice of 18 lemons, and complete the sherbet with a strong infusion of green tea; add the oleo-saccharum, and equal proportions of pale brandy and pine-apple rum, according to strength desired.

Ponche à la Parisienne.—Boil in ½ pint of water 1 lb. of sugar; when it comes to the thread, add the oleo-saccharum of 1 lemon and juice of 2, 1 ½ pint of brandy, and ½ pint of rum; let this heat, but not boil; pour it into a hot bowl; set fire to it; stir it well, and pour into glasses while blazing.

Henry Knight's Punch.—Quart of tea, ½ pint mock arrack (Vauxhall nectar), gill of brandy, juice of 2 lemons, thin peel of one, gill of Scotch whisky, and tablespoonful of apple or quince jelly; mix, and drink hot.

Orbell's Punch.—Drop 1 drop each of essence of cinnamon, pimento, cloves, ginger, neroli, and nutmeg on a piece of sugar; digest this in a gill of rum; add pint of sherry, pint of port, and juice of 2 lemons; sugar to taste; water as may be desired.

Imperial Punch.—Cream of tartar 2 oz., juice and peel of 2 lemons, 6 quarts of water, ½ pint pine-apple rum.

Orange Punch.—Strain the juice of 6 (St. Michael) oranges; rub sufficiently off the rind of a Seville (or Mandarin) orange to impart a pleasing flavour; add 1 drop of essence of neroli, pint of brandy, pint of orange-shrub; sweeten to taste, and add as much liquor as desired.

Apple Punch.—Into a jug lay slices of apples and lemons alternately; strew between each layer some powdered sugar-candy; pour over them a bottle of either Claret, Chablis, or Roussillon, and ½ gill of brandy; in four hours strain, with pressure.

Essence of Punch.—The oleo-saccharum of 2 Seville oranges

and 1 lemon; mix with the strained juice of 2 lemons and
2 Seville oranges; add 5 oz. loaf or barley sugar.

Into a jar put 1 bottle of brandy, ½ bottle of rum, ¼
ditto of shrub, and 1 pinch of flowers of benzoin when
well amalgamated; mix together when required for use;
add liquor as desired.

Gin Punch à la Garrick.—Rub the ambrosial essence of 1
lemon on a 2 oz. lump of loaf-sugar, which dissolve in
the juice of same; add ½ pint of gin, wine-glass full of
Maraschino, pint of shaven ice, and 2 bottles of soda-water.

Gin Punch à la Terrington.—Rub the rind of ½ lemon with a
4 oz. lump of sugar; add the juice of 3 lemons (strained), 1
pint of good gin, wine-glassful of Chartreuse (green), pint
of shaven ice, 1 bottle of German seltzer water.

Gin Punch à la J. Day.—The oleo-saccharum of 1 and strained
juice of 2 lemons, pint of Old Tom, wine-glass of Curaçoa,
teaspoonful of sugar, 1 sprig of mint, pint of crushed Lake
ice, 2 bottles of aërated lemonade or soda-water.

Gin Punch à la Burroughs.—Juice of 1 lemon, 1 gill of
pine-apple syrup, 1 pint of gin, 1 quart of tea (green). If
preferred as a cool punch, use broken ice instead of tea.

Gin Punch, or Spider.—Gill of gin, bottle of aërated lemonade, lump of Lake ice: a liqueur-glass of citronelle is an
improvement.

Gin Punch à la Gooch.—Pint of Geneva, gill of Kirschwasser,
bottle of sparkling champagne, quart of seltzer or Vichy
water.

Gin Punch for Bottling.—The oleo-saccharum of 3 lemons,
dissolved in 1 pint of lemon-juice; add ½ gill essence of
Angelica, and 3 pints of good gin; ½ pint calves-foot jelly;

sweeten to taste; dilute, when required for use, with liquor.

Gin Punch à la Fuller.—Pint of Kentish cherry-juice, 1 drop essence of bitter almonds, 2 pints of good unsweetened gin; mix; sweeten to taste; add water or shaven ice if required.

Whisky Punch à la Taylor.—The oleo-saccharum of 1 Seville or Mandarin orange, 1 tablespoonful of tamarinds, ½ pint of lemon-juice, and 1 pint of whisky; strain clear; add boiling water and sugar to taste.

Whisky Punch.—Juice and peel of 1 lemon in ½ pint of whisky, sweetened to taste; water *ad libitum.*

Whisky Punch à la Barrett.—½ pint of whisky, teaspoonful of guava or apple jelly, ½ pint of boiling water.

Ponche à la Romaine, à la Stewart.—Pint of orange-juice (sweetened), bottle of sparkling Moselle, ½ gill of rum, whites of 3 or 4 eggs, according to size, whisked into a stiff froth; mix in freezing-pot, using the spatula well; when frozen, serve in coloured glasses.

Ponche à la Romaine, à la Brunning.—Quart of lemon-water ice; add teaspoonful of essence of ginger; the frothed whites of 4 eggs, with 3 oz. of sugar (powdered); put in freezing-pot; add, while working, wine-glass of rum, and two of sherry or champagne; serve as given.

Ponche à la Romaine, à la Montrose.—Quart of cherry-water ice, bottle of Moselle, wine-glass of Kirschwasser, ditto of noyeau, wine-glass of gin; work till well frozen; add 5 whites of eggs of Italian meringue paste; serve in coloured glasses.

Ponche à la Romaine, à la Jones.—Pint of noyeau ice; gill of Curaçoa; pint of orange wine; 4 whites of eggs, beaten up in a froth, with 4 oz. pounded sugar; freeze and serve.

Ponche à la Romaine, à la Hastings.—Quart of pine-apple ice; clear lemon-juice, to taste; bottle of sparkling Moselle or Champagne, wine-glass of Chartreuse, ditto of peach brandy, whites of 6 eggs, beaten up with 6 oz. pounded sugar.

Ponche à la Romaine, à la Hall.—1 pint pine-apple syrup, 2 drops essence of orange-peel, 1 drop of ambergris, pint of dry sherry, pint of cider, 4 whites of eggs of Italian meringue paste; while freezing, add ¼ pint of rum; if too stiff, thin with cider; serve in coloured glasses.

Ponche à la Romaine, à la Jeanes.—1 quart lemon ice, whites of 3 eggs, 3 oz. powdered sugar, 1 glass Cognac brandy, 1 glass best rum, ½ pint champagne, 2 glasses dry sherry; stir the lemon ice in a basin; add the frothed whites, beaten up into a stiff paste, with the pounded sugar; mix the spirit and wine; freeze in freezing-pot, and serve in coloured glasses.

Ponche à la Romaine, à la Somerset.—Quart of lemon-water ice, pint of Amontillado, liqueur-glass of Chartreuse, bottle of Champagne, frothed whites of 4 eggs, 4 oz. of sugar. Proceed as shown in previous formula.

Ponche à la Romaine, à la Reid.—Quart of lemon-water ice, gill of rum, pint of Chablis, the whisked whites of 4 eggs, with 4 oz. powdered sugar; freeze by the usual method.

TABLE OF WEIGHTS AND MEASURES

Thimbleful = 30 drops
Teaspoonful = 60 drops
Dessert-spoonful = 2 fluid drachms
Tablespoonful = 4 fluid drachms (½ oz.)
Wine-glassful = 2 fluid oz. (⅛ of a wine-pint)
Tumblerful = 8 fluid oz. (½ pint)
4 gills, or noggins = 1 pint
2 pints = 1 quart
4 quarts = 1 gallon
63 gallons = 1 hogshead
84 gallons = 1 puncheon

APOTHECARIES' WEIGHT
20 grains = 1 scruple
3 scruples = 1 drachm
8 drachms = 1 ounce
12 ounces = 1 pound

AVOIRDUPOIS WEIGHT
16 drachms = 1 ounce
16 ounces = 1 pound
Pinch of herbs = 1 drachm

Handful = 10 drachms